Samuel Edward Dawson, Royal Society of Canada

The Lines of Demarcation of Pope Alexander VI

and the Treaty of Tordesillas A.D. 1493 and 1494

Samuel Edward Dawson, Royal Society of Canada

The Lines of Demarcation of Pope Alexander VI
and the Treaty of Tordesillas A.D. 1493 and 1494

ISBN/EAN: 9783337091354

Printed in Europe, USA, Canada, Australia, Japan

Cover: Foto ©Lupo / pixelio.de

More available books at **www.hansebooks.com**

FROM THE TRANSACTIONS OF THE ROYAL SOCIETY OF CANADA

SECOND SERIES—1899-1900

VOLUME V   SECTION II

ENGLISH HISTORY, LITERATURE, ARCHÆOLOGY, ETC.

THE LINES OF DEMARCATION

OF

POPE ALEXANDER VI.

AND THE

TREATY OF TORDESILLAS

A.D. 1493 and 1494

By SAMUEL EDWARD DAWSON Lit.D. (Laval)

FOR SALE BY

J. HOPE & SONS, OTTAWA; THE COPP-CLARK CO., TORONTO

1899

VII.—*The Line of Demarcation of Pope Alexander VI. in A. D. 1493 and that of the Treaty of Tordesillas in A.D. 1494; with an inquiry concerning the Metrology of Ancient and Mediæval Times.*

By SAMUEL EDWARD DAWSON, Litt. D. (Laval).

(Read May 26, 1899.)

CONTENTS.

APPENDICES.

1.—INTRODUCTION.

While during the last five years scholars in the north have been discussing the voyages of the Cabots ; in the south, an acrimonious controversy was carried on by politicians concerning the coasts of Venezuela and Guiana, the scenes of the discoveries of Columbus, Hojeda and Pinzon. The question has now been settled, but it would seem that civilization has not gained as much, during the last four hundred years, as might have been expected, inasmuch as political recklessness nearly resulted in bringing on a war between the United States and Great Britain. Patient statesmanship averted that crime and the controversy was at last referred to a tribunal of arbitration and a great calamity to civilization was prevented.

The diplomatic documents cited in support of the claim of Venezuela go back to the very earliest years of the discovery of the New World. With the direct question of the boundary between Venezuela and British Guiana, now happily settled, the present paper is not concerned: but indirect questions were raised, interesting to every student of early American history, and therefore, of early Canadian history, for the history of Canada strikes its roots as deep down into the centuries as does the history of any part of the continent. Before Columbus touched the mainland near the *Boca de la Sierpe,* Cabot had coasted the shores of Newfoundland and Nova Scotia.

The main object of this paper is to elucidate the line of demarcation drawn in 1493 between the Old World and the New by Pope Alexander VI. and its modification by treaty the following year. Not much has been written upon this subject in English. There is a very excellent article by Prof. Edward G. Bourne in the *Report of the American Historical Association* for 1891, and a recent volume by Mr. Henry Harrisse (*Diplomatic History of America,* London, 1897), full of research, as all his books are ; but beyond these the student must have recourse to other languages than English if he should seek information of value concerning what has been called, somewhat hastily, that "absurd act of assumption." We shall find, on closer inquiry, that we have no right to a patent for the idea of an international tribunal of arbitration. There was one in permanent session in 1493 ; and, by its decision, war was then averted between the two foremost nations in Christendom. We shall see, moreover, that although the ownership of half the world was involved war was not then so imminent as it was

recently between England and the United States ; not because of anything in dispute between them, but on account of a petty territory
claimed by a third government, and in assertion of a speculative proposition in international law of recent invention and doubtful author-
ship.

The case for Venezuela was based primarily on the Bull of Pope
Alexander and upon discovery. Without entering into the controversy
it may be observed, that the argument proves too much ; for the whole
of the present United States fell within the Spanish demarcation and,
from where Cabot's voyage ended, the whole coast of the Atlantic was
first discovered, and ceremonial possession was taken, for Spain. The
British take their title in Guiana from the Dutch, and the United
States take their title from the British ; so that it is not easy to build
an argument on discovery and upon the Bull of 1493 without involving
some considerable portions of the United States.

While these questions may however be considered as settled it will
interest the student to recall the fact that, in these northern seas, the
line of demarcation was supposed to cut our coast and that Nova Scotia
and Newfoundland fell to Portugal. This has been incidentally referred
to in previous papers ; but, inasmuch as the papal Bulls of 1493 and
the Treaty of Tordesillas of 1494 are within the scope of our history,
it is not lost labour to inquire what these documents were and what was
their meaning.

Nothing is more trite than to insist upon the importance of treating each period of history from its own point of view ; but nothing is
more difficult. In recent controversies on early American history it
has been often forgotten that Western Europe was Roman Catholic
when America was discovered, and that, although the secular head of
the Holy Roman Empire had lost his relative importance, the authority
of its spiritual head was still unchallenged. Latin was, in effect, a
living language—the living language of the services of the Church and
a living language for all educated men throughout Europe. The
Romance languages themselves had not diverged so widely as now, either
from each other or from their common source ; and the barriers of
nationality were not raised nearly so high then as they are at the present
day. Those who gibbet Sebastian Cabot as a scoundrel and traitor for
changing his service, forget that the great sailors of his day changed
masters without reproach and that soldiers and statesmen frequently
did the same. No one blames Philippe de Comines, who was born a
Burgundian subject and served in the council of Charles the Bold,
for passing over into equally confidential and important employments

under his mortal enemy, Louis XI. of France; but Cabot, an Italian, born in Venice, is judged as if he had been a captain in the French navy who had sought employment from the Emperor of Germany. This is a misleading anachronism, for the present exaggerated antagonism of nationalities is of comparatively recent growth and received its chief impetus in the religious wars which followed in the sixteenth century.

The same tendency to anachronism has affected the interpretation of the old charts. If the early sailors had possessed sufficient knowledge they would have made more accurate maps; but they had neither the information nor the instruments necessary, therefore the secret of longitude was hidden from them. All their longitudinal distances were calculated by dead reckoning; and the log line, even, was not in use until 1521, but their maps are now often measured in millimetres as if they were the products of an admiralty survey. Elaborate arguments have been founded upon the trend of their coast lines, without considering that their maps were drawn to compass bearings, and ours are always drawn to the true meridian. The conditions of the age in which they lived made it possible for the sailors of all the western nations to calculate their distances by a uniform customary league; but that league was not the admiralty league of three minutes of the Equator nor the English land league of three statute miles.

The present paper then, although it may have been suggested by the Venezuelan controversy, will not discuss the boundary of British Guiana. Its object is to throw light upon our own history by a detailed examination of the Bulls of Pope Alexander VI. and the pretensions based upon them. The distances specified in the Bull and in the treaty lead to a discussion of the nautical measures of length in use at that time and the Portuguese names still clinging to our coasts bear witness to the belief that the line of demarcation cut the northeastern coast of America, somewhere in the present province of Nova Scotia. All these subjects are of interest, since they bear upon the true interpretation of the early maps and the elucidation of the historical geography of our Atlantic coast.

II.—INTERNATIONAL LAW IN 1493.

It has been stated by writers of great weight that Grotius laid the foundation of international law as it is now understood. This means that, in the application of the principles of international law, references seldom go further back than to the exhaustive work of Grotius, published at Paris in 1625. It does not mean that international law did

not exist before Grotius, or that he originated its principles. The most
cursory glance at his great work, *De Jure Belli*, will show that all his
illustrations were drawn from Greek, Roman and Jewish history, and it
will be found, on perusal, that his principles are derived from natural
law or the law of nature as laid down by the Roman lawyers, upon the
Roman civil law as found in the *Corpus Juris*, upon the works of the
more philosophical of the Christian Fathers, upon the Synodical Canons
recorded in ecclesiastical history and upon the Divine law as revealed
in the Bible. Grotius does not, himself, pretend to anything else. He
was born in 1583, ninety years after the discovery of America, and to
attempt therefore, to pass judgment on the Bull of 1493 in the light of
our present notions, is an absurd anachronism. Grotius goes further,
and, while justly claiming the merit of his work, refers to authors who
had preceded him who, as he says, were "partly Divines and partly
Doctors of Law." If, therefore, we put aside the conventional law or
treaty law of nations, it will be seen that modern international law is
founded on the Roman law and on the Canon law, which latter was
carried over all Europe by the Roman Church ; for even in England up
to the time of Edward III. the Lord Chancellor was always an ecclesiastic. In commenting on this point, Sir Henry Maine observes[1] that "it
" is astonishing how small a proportion the additions made to inter-
" national law since Grotius's day bear to the ingredients which have
" been simply taken from the most ancient stratum of the Roman
" *Jus Gentium.*" This *Jus Gentium* is the law of nature applicable to
all human beings, and therefore to nations collectively, and is eloquently said by Cicero[2] to be "That law which was neither a thing con-
" trived by the genius of man, nor established by any decree of the
" people ; but a certain eternal principle, which governs the entire
" universe, wisely commanding what is right and prohibiting what is
" wrong. . . . Therefore, the true and supreme law, whose commands and
" prohibitions are equally authoritative, is the right reason of the
" Sovereign Jupiter."

These things being so, it is somewhat flippant for the *London
Times* to characterize the citation of the Bull of 1493, in the Venezuela
dispute, as "comical" or "absurd." It was good law *pro tanto*, for
where else was there, at that time, a court so competent, by learning or
tradition, to decide questions which, in their essence, depended on the
Roman or Canon law as the Court of Rome ? Nor could there, *a priori*,
be conceived one more likely to be impartial ; for the Pope had no
sailors through whom he could discover and claim for himself new
lands. Flings at the private character of Alexander VI. are only pre-
texts for avoiding argument. We have to do with him in this paper

only as a geographer and as judge in a court in a secular matter ; nor
have we even to discuss his authority ; because he was, at least in this
case, a court of consensual jurisdiction. The popes could see, as
Grotius afterwards saw, "such license of going to war as even barbarous
"nations may be ashamed of, that men take arms greedily for light
"causes, or none at all." No one at that time impugned their authority,
and why should they have recused themselves from an office, or shirked
a duty, so clearly incumbent on them in their quality as head of the
Christian commonwealth ?

The conception was, indeed, lofty and most Christian. The heart
of every earnest thinker must go forth in sympathy to the man who,
in the isolation of an autocratic throne, has, in these latter days,
dreamed such a dream as the institution of a court of supreme international appeal. Such a position the popes did in fact occupy at the
period of the discovery of America and, as is pointed out by Bryce,[3]
" they were excellently fitted for it, by the respect which the sacredness
" of their office commanded ; by their control of the tremendous
" weapons of excommunication and interdict ; above all by their ex-
" emption from those narrowing influences of place, or blood or personal
" interest which it would be their chiefest duty to resist in others."
For reasons beyond the scope of our argument this was soon to cease ;
but in A.D. 1493, Christendom was still conceived to be an organized
body of Christian states, of which the Pope was the spiritual head.
There was, therefore, an innate fitness in the lawyers and doctors of
the civil and canon law at the *Curia Romana* to deal with broad questions of natural and divine law or universal justice extending over independent nations. The proceedings at Rome were, in matters of international interest, not arbitrary but formal and technical ; for there
were resident representatives there of all the powers of Christendom.
During the period of their power the popes had often helped the weak
against the strong and had often strenuously laboured for that "truce
of God," which, even in present times, can alone avert the impending
Armageddon. We learn from Sir Henry Maine[4] that Bentham was so
impressed with the confusion attending the modern views of right to
territories by discovery and occupancy, that he went out of his way to
eulogize this very Bull of Pope Alexander; and Maine himself adds that,
although praises of any act of papal authority may seem grotesque in
a writer like Bentham, "it may be doubted, whether the arrangement
" of Pope Alexander is absurder in principle than the rule of public
" law which gave half a continent to the monarch whose servants had
" fulfilled the conditions required by Roman jurisprudence for the ac-

" quisition of property in a valuable object which could be covered by
" the hand."

Modern diplomacy is not in a position to regard as "comical" or
"ridiculous" the attempt of the Pope, in 1493, to draw a line of demarcation through the ocean in the interests of peace between the only
powers which were then concerning themselves with discovery and
extension, for, translated into the very latest diplomatic form of speech,
it was nothing else than the delimitation of "spheres of influence,"
such as, during the last few years, have resulted in the partition of the
continent of Africa. The doctrine of "Hinterland," is the old principle under a new name. It is the principle which pervaded the old
charters of the American colonies and made them to extend their
claims from sea to sea. As it was then, so it is now ; enormous regions
are being marked off upon the map, regions whither white travellers
have barely penetrated and containing immense numbers of people who
have never seen a European. These are being allotted to one power or
another, without any more rational grounds then were the Western or
Eastern Indies in 1493 ; and from time to time a Fashoda incident
crops up to demonstrate the absence of any governing principle.

It has been argued that the perfect equality of each sovereign
state, without regard to its size or strength, is a modern principle of
international law. That however is doubtful, for it seems in the case
of weak nations to depend rather upon the mutual jealousies of the
greater states. Grotius although, as before stated, he mentioned in
his preface the names of some of his predecessors in the field of international law, did not mention Francis a Victoria, a learned theologian
of Salamanca, who in two chapters of his work, *Relectiones Theologicæ*,
published first at Lyons in 1559, and then at Salamanca in 1565, went
far beyond Grotius and even surpassed the writers of the present day
in his humane and liberal views. The book is very rare, but Hallam
(Hist. Lit. Vol. 2) gives an account of it and there is a more detailed
analysis in Salomon's *L'Occupation des Territoires sans Maitre*. The
chapters bearing on the present question are those entitled *de Indis* and
de Jure Belli, and the fact that such views were at that date publicly
expressed by an ecclesiastical professor of high repute, is worthy of
serious attention. He maintained that the Spaniards had no more right
to the Indies by discovery than the Indians would have had to Spain if
they had discovered Spain—that, by public and private law, the Indians
were as justly owners of their own lands as if they were Christians—
that the Indians did not lose their rights because they were unbelievers,
since they had not had the opportunity of knowing the true faith—
that Jews and Saracens who were hostile to Christianity retained their

lands and that nominal Christian princes did so also, though their morals were often not so good as those of the Indians, and moreover, that God bestowed his gifts, as he made his sun to rise and his rain to fall, upon the evil and the good. Proceeding with relentless logic, the learned professor demonstrated that the Pope could have no possible right over the lands of these people, since the dominion of Christ himself was spiritual, and, if they were heathen, then still less would be the power of the Pope over them ; for they would not even be subject to his spiritual authority and that no just war could be waged against them on that account. These views, as to the power of the Pope in matters purely temporal, held as they were in the great Spanish university of Salamanca, will be referred to later on ; but at present it must be observed that he still made out to justify the Bull of Pope Alexander, but by two arguments so modern and "up to date," that they might emanate from a Mission Board at New York, or a board of directors at London. If, he argues, these Indians allow the missionaries freely to preach the gospel and meet their efforts only by indifference, they stand in their right ; but if they resist with violence or persecute the neophytes, there will be a just cause of war. That is the argument for the Mission Boards, but the other is no less happy. Every Christian nation, he argued, has an absolute right of commerce with every other Christian nation and to sail its ships along their coasts ; that right exists therefore towards every pagan nation as well, and, if resisted, there is also a just cause of war. Now we can see the right of the British ships to open the ports of China and the American ships the ports of Japan ; but the learned professor of three centuries ago is still in advance of us, for we evade his conclusions by coasting laws and prohibitive tariffs. If the Chinese and Japanese had admitted our ships under similar laws one would like to call back the shade of this most excellent ecclesiastic and ask his opinion, whether a prohibitive tariff was not a prohibitive law.

The reference of such territorial questions to the Pope was moreover rational ; since geographical knowledge was nowhere cultivated with so much curiosity and intelligence as at Rome, because of the universality of the claims of the Roman See. The Canon law required the attendance of bishops, at definite intervals, at the Court of Rome, and they were bound to make certain reports through their metropolitans. By these channels the Popes became, on geographical matters, the best informed men in Europe.

Upon this subject there has been a great deal of *ad captandum* writing ; for, while it is quite true that current opinion in the middle ages upon geography was crude and absurd, it is also true that the

doctrine of the sphericity of the earth, as taught by the Greek geographers, was held by the greater minds within the Church and never
authoritatively rebuked.   Herein is the essential unfairness of books like
President Andrew D. White's *Warfare of Science*.   He holds the Roman
Church responsible for the sputterings of Cosmas Indicopleustes.   But
that irritable religionist was not a churchman by training, and, although
in late life he became a monk in Egypt, he was a merchant, a traveller
and a sailor for the greater part of his life—he was never a priest.   His
travels were extensive and his observations upon what he actually saw
were valuable ; but his *Christian Topography* was written in Greek, in
the time of Justinian.   To make the Roman Church responsible for
his extravagances is not fair disputation.   The belief in the sphericity
of the earth was by no means general in Greek and Roman times.   The
Epicureans laughed at it as a vagary of Pythagoras, and those who, in
all ages, are called "common-sense people," did not believe it any more
than Cosmas,—though they might have been pagans.   In Chapter VII.
of Plutarch's treatise, *On the Apparent Face in the Moon's Orb*, the
theory is ridiculed by one of the speakers.   No doubt in the middle ages,
as in ancient times, the belief was common that the world was flat ;
but it was not a doctrine of the church.   The passage so often cited
from St. Augustine merely states that even " if it be supposed or
" scientifically demonstrated that the world is of a round and spherical
" form, it does not *logically* follow that the other side of the world is
" peopled, seeing that nobody has been there to see and that it may be
" all water or, if indeed land, may be bare of inhabitants."   The logic
is unanswerable and the general opinion was that there were no antipodes ; though Columbus, than whom there never was a more fervent
Catholic, held to the contrary.   There were two systems current.   One
held, with Pomponius Mela to the notion of a southern hemisphere
separated from ours by an ocean impassable from heat, and the other
held with Ptolemy, the belief in a southern continent extending from
Africa to Eastern Asia and inclosing the Indian Ocean.   During the
dissolution and re-crystallization of society there was very little opportunity to think about science and, for the masses, the times were indeed dark ; but, and the exception is fatal to President White's thesis,
such science as there was existed in the cloister alone ; and that of
necessity was the case, for there, in those turbulent days, was the sole
refuge for a quiet thinker and in the church was the only career for a
man of great intellect but of humble birth ; because the highest position in it was not limited by class or race or family.   Thus it came
about that the church attained such power and that with the exception
of our own Alfred, laymen left so slight a record in the world of letters.

There was nothing to prevent them becoming scholars had they been so inclined. Albert the Great, Bishop of Bollstadt, lectured publicly at Cologne, and recorded in his writings his belief in the existence of antipodes. So did Friar Bacon and, from his writings, Cardinal d'Ailly adopted similar opinions. The *Imago Mundi* of d'Ailly was the abiding solace of Columbus in his passionate struggles and it was also the chief source of his cosmological knowledge ; since from it, chiefly, he gathered his knowledge of the theories and conclusions of the Greek and Arabian geographers. It is not true that the theories of Columbus were antagonized especially by churchmen. On the contrary, the Dominican monks at Salamanca were in advance of the lay professors in their scientific views. Those who mainly assisted Columbus to obtain access to the Catholic sovereigns were Fray Juan Perez (Franciscan) Prior of La Rabida, Fray Hernando Talavera (Dominican) Prior of Prado and Confessor to the Queen, Fray Diego Deza, Professor of Theology at Salamanca, and Cardinal de Mendoza, who was a minister of the Crown. It was not the scholars nor the churchmen, *qua* churchmen, who opposed Columbus ; but the "clear headed practical common sense folk," of all classes ; supported by the men, and they are not all dead yet, who have an infallible gift for finding their own notions in the Scriptures. Writing in 1498, from St. Domingo to the King and Queen, Columbus expresses his gratitude; "all others," he writes, "who had thought of the matter, or heard it spoken of, unani- "mously treated it with contempt, with the exception of two friars, " who always remained constant in their belief in its practicability."

It is no part of the object of this paper to discuss the beliefs and dogmas of the church ; but it is due to geographical science to say that it is simply untrue that Pope Alexander, as President White asserts, (*Warfare of Science*, Appleton, 1876, p. 19) laid down "a line of de- " marcation upon the earth as upon a flat disk," and it will be seen, as we proceed, that it is also untrue that " this was hailed as an exercise " of divinely illuminated power in the church " (p. 20). Globes were not in the least uncommon then. The year Columbus sailed, Martin Behaim made a large globe still to be seen at Nuremburg. Long before that (in 1474) Columbus had sent a globe to Toscanelli at Florence, and we read of a globe before 1497 upon which John Cabot taught his son the properties of the sphere. It may readily be supposed that all the globes then in existence are not spoken of in the books. It is not necessary to think, moreover, with Mr. Harrisse° that the Pope was probably basing his partition upon a plane chart, when he sent the Bull to the Spanish monarchs. It was quite unnecessary, because the line was clearly enough indicated—north and south, from pole to pole, one hundred leagues from the Azores or other Portuguese islands. The new discovery of necessity destroyed the value of all previous charts and it was not in the least necessary that the Pope, or his lawyers, should waste any portion of the very short time spent in preparing the Bull in measuring off a hundred leagues upon a chart of any kind. As for President White's "flat disk," the very words of the Bull, "from the "Arctic pole to the Antarctic pole," preclude the notion.

Again the popes were, in geographical questions, of necessity in advance of their age ; for, during the thirteenth and fourteenth centuries, they had been sending envoys—simple monks for the most part—to the far east to the Tartar emperors, who had broken down the barriers of Mohammedan exclusiveness, and in that way their knowledge of the world had been greatly extended. Moreover, they favoured geographical study. The first translation of Ptolemy into Latin, in 1409, was dedicated to Pope Alexander V. Pope Nicholas V. commanded the first translation of Strabo, and the first printed edition was dedicated to Pope Paul II. In 1478, the first complete edition of Ptolemy was published and it was printed at Rome and dedicated to Pope Sixtus IV. Æneas Sylvius, afterwards Pope Pius II., wrote a work on cosmography and a copy still exists with annotations on the margin in the admiral's own handwriting. The *Decades* of Peter Martyr are mostly letters to popes to keep them informed of the discoveries being made by Spanish and Portuguese sailors. For these and many other reasons a question of cosmography could, at that time, be decided better at Rome than anywhere else.

Whatever be their form, the true nature of these Bulls is an award and not a donation ; for they are all drawn subject to a right by discovery. The respective "spheres of influence" of Spain and Portugal were delimited ; but the grant to Spain is made "upon condition that "no other Christian king or prince has actual possession of the islands "and mainlands found or that shall be found" before the Christmas last past. Nor need the learned President take exception to the words, "of our own free will and certain knowledge and in the plenitude of "our apostolic power." There are similar words in all documents of that nature by others than popes, for instance, in the patent and ratification of privileges to Columbus (April 23, 1497), after stating in the preamble that the power of the sovereigns is derived from "God alone, "whose place they supply in temporal affairs," the grant reads "of our "own proper motion, certain knowledge and royal absolute power." The wording is nearly identical and so is the material form ; for it is a lay Bull, "sealed with a *leaden seal hanging by threads of coloured silk.*" The principle is the same in the wording of such documents even now.

The authority is usually referred to and in a republic would read—in virtue of the authority committed to me by the people, etc., etc. It is merely the substitution of the will of the majority for Divine Providence.

In despite of the form of donation it will appear that, even in those days, the title went by discovery. The reason of the request for the special Bull is shown later on, and we learn from Herrera that, when asking for it, the Catholic sovereigns did not compromise their prerogative ; but stated that "most learned scholars in Spain thought " that the application for a grant of territory already in their possession " was unnecessary." No other decision was open to the Pope, seeing that Spain gave clear proof of discovery and of possession taken. These circumstances are recited in the Bull. In those days, title by discovery required a formal taking possession in the name of the sovereign with ceremonies, frequently of a religious character, as well as by unfurling and saluting a flag. There has been very little change in succeeding years. As the European nations began to overflow and unoccupied regions were seized, the extent of territory covered by a settlement grew narrower, but the presently existing doctrine of "effectual occupation" was not formulated until the conference at Berlin, in 1884, when Germany waked up to the fact that the world had been almost occupied while she had been busy in consolidating her national unity. There is not so much "presumption" in the Bull as in the charter of Henry VII. to Cabot three years later. He granted power to "saile to all parts, " countreys, and seas of the East, of the West and of the North, to " seeke out, discover and finde whatsoever isles, regions, etc., of the " heathen and infidels whatsoever they be and in what part of the " worlde soever they be." Then Henry gives the grantees power to " subdue, occupy and possess all such townes, cities, castles and isles of " them found, which they are to occupy and possess as our vassals, etc.. " giving unto us the rule, title and jurisdiction of the same villages, " townes, etc., and firme land so found," and in the same lofty style Henry disposes of the regions to be discovered as if they were his property or his by right of his Crown. An unprejudiced comparison will compel the admission that Pope Alexander was the less "arrogant and presumptuous" of the two ; for he at least assigned a defensible reason : namely, the conversion of the infidels and the carrying of the gospel into all lands. This, in fact, it was his proper function to see to ; for he was at the head of the only mission board then in existence. For centuries after it was not thought that a non-Christian people were capable of sovereignty and proprietorship. Indeed, the question is hardly settled yet in the case of pagan nations. I am not discussing the principle ; I am simply asserting that it still survives, and that in the light of many occurrences in the Pacific and in eastern seas, it might be well to examine our own consciences without dissembling before throwing stones at Pope Alexander on this account.

While arguing for the validity of the Bull of 1493 the Venezuelan counsel have greatly overstated the submissiveness of the English monarchs of those days and the historical instances of Mr. Harrisse, whose *Diplomatic History of America* seems to have been prepared for the case, have led them into error. While it is true that the Bull *Laudabiliter* is authentic, it is necessary to read it in its own terms, when it will appear, as Dr. Lingard[7] long ago observed, that the Pope " Adrian, by this instrument, avoids the usual language of feudal " grants; he merely signifies his acquiescence in the king's project; " he is willing that Henry should enter Ireland and *be acknowledged as* " *Lord by the natives.*" The submission of Henry cited as having occurred at Avranches is not accepted as historical by English authorities; but even if the circumstance actually occurred, as stated, the agreement is admitted to have been a private one by those who assert that it was made. Being then, at the utmost, secret and made without the consent of the barons, whatever binding effect it might have upon Henry himself, it was invalid as against the realm of England.

An intimate knowledge of the laws and ceremonial language of Spain has probably prevented Senor Rafael Seijas from incorporating Mr. Harrisse's sixth chapter in the "case." He could not take so seriously the oration of filial allegiance and submission in which the envoys of Ferdinand and Isabella, on an errand of congratulation to the newly elected Pope, "lay at the feet of His Holiness, all they possess on " earth and on the seas; not only their kingdoms, treasures, fleets and " armies, but also their sons and royal persons." This must be taken to mean only obedience in spiritual matters. Mr. Harrisse's ideas of the relations between the temporal and spiritual powers would have shocked every lawyer and statesman in Spain and nine-tenths of the clergy also.

It would lead me from my theme to discuss a subject so vast in its literature and so important. I shall, however, enable the reader to form, for himself, an opinion as to the extent of the submission in strictly temporal matters of the monarchs of those days by letting them speak for themselves. The following is an extract from a letter by William I., who had just conquered England, to Pope Gregory VII.— the great Hildebrand of Canossa memory—and William had received a consecrated banner for his expedition from Gregory's predecessor.

" To Gregory, the most excellent Pastor of the Holy Church, William, by " the grace of God, King of England and Duke of Normandy, sends health and " friendship.

" Your legate, Hubert, religious father, has admonished me on your part to
" do homage to you and your successors, and to think better of the money which
" my predecessors were accustomed to send to the Roman Church. Of these
" demands, one I have granted ; the other I have refused. Homage I would not
" nor will I do. For I did not promise it myself ; nor can I learn that it was ever
" done by my predecessors to yours," etc., etc.

Then he promises to send the usual money.

The next letter is from the barons of England to Pope Boniface
VIII., (the writer of the " Unam Sanctam.") who had declared that
Scotland was a fief of the Holy See and had summoned Edward I. to
desist from invasion and plead the matter in the Roman Court.

" To the most holy father in Christ, the Lord Boniface, by divine Providence,
" chief bishop of the Holy Roman Church, John, Earl of Warren, and one hun-
" dred and five other barons, send greeting.
" It is well known to us and to many others, most holy father, that the
" kingdom of Scotland never did, nor does, by any right whatever, belong, in
" temporals, to the Roman Church. Nor have the Kings of England, on account
" of the independent pre-eminence of their royal dignity, and a custom at all
" times inviolably observed, ever pleaded, or been bound to plead, with respect to
" their right to the kingdom aforesaid, or to their other temporal rights, before
" any ecclesiastical or secular judge whatsoever," etc., etc.

The barons then go on to say that even if the king were disposed
to plead they would not permit him to do so ; as it would be to " the
" manifest disherison of the rights of the Crown of England and sub-
" version of the laws, charters and customs inherited from their
" fathers."

In the face of these two letters the argument as to the submission
of the English kings based by the Venezuelan counsel on Mr. Harrisse's
book falls to the ground. One more letter, and this, from the very
King Ferdinand the Catholic, who sent the embassy of obedience to
which Mr. Harrisse devotes a chapter, will suffice to show the difference between obedience in temporal and in spiritual matters. Ferdinand was King of Naples, as well as of Aragon, and the Pope had
served upon his vice-roy at Naples, a Brief without sending it first to
be examined and receive the royal *placet* before publication ; according to the fundamental laws of these kingdoms. The King writes to
his vice-roy and after reciting the circumstances, he continues :

" All this has not a little excited our anger and indignation ; and we are
" equally surprised at and displeased with you ; that, considering the importance
" of the case and the prejudice which our royal dignity suffered from the act of
" the apostolical messenger, which is a violence against all right, never practised
" against any king or viceroy of my kingdom," etc., etc.

Then, after expressing his indignation that the Pope's messenger
had not been instantly hanged, the King goes on to show how the act
might be cancelled, as follows :—

" You must also use all possible diligence to seize the messenger who pre-
" sented the said Brief ; if you can get hold of him, he must retract the presenta-
" tion which he made you of the Brief, and renounce it by a formal act ; after
" which you will have him immediately hanged," etc., etc.

These letters cover the period of the greatest height of papal
power, and it is strange that a Venezuelan statesman familiar with
the fundamental law of Spain, could have fallen into such an error.
Mr. Harrisse has evidently not turned his attention to this branch of
history for he wrote in 1892 in his *Discovery of America* (p. 54).
" Nay, whenever a new pope was elected all the Christian kings had
" again to do homage for their possessions, old and recent." It is a
surprising statement.   Claims were in past ages sometimes made by
popes and extremists, whom Dante (*De Monarchia*) calls "decretalists,"
but no such general claims as these extending to all kingdoms were made
and, beyond doubt, no such acts of homage were ever performed.

Although the remarks immediately preceding may seem to lead
away from the main subject, they do not in reality. It is necessary
to clear away these misconceptions concerning the early documents of
our history. The Venezuelan dispute was not settled by the Bull or
by the principle of discovery ; but by the occurrences of the Dutch
occupation. In 1875, the dispute between Spain and Germany for
the Caroline islands was referred to Pope Leo XIII., and he decided for
Spain ; but he did not go upon the title by discovery, nor did he even
allude to the Bull of his predecessor. He based his award upon repeated acts of occupation by Spain down to the very moment the dispute arose. In 1493, circumstances were very different, and while we
must take exception to such statements as the preceding, concerning
the submission of European princes generally, or English princes
specially, in temporals to the Roman See, we must concede to the Pon-
tiffs a position as international judges if upon no higher ground than
upon the ground of consensual jurisdiction.

III.—The Outward Form.

Before proceeding to consider the papal Bulls bearing on this
question, it is necessary to dwell for a moment upon the outward form
of these documents ; because, in Protestant countries, vague notions
often prevail concerning them and also because, in his *Diplomatic
History*, Mr. Harrisse has treated these American Bulls so incau-
tiously as to throw new stumbling blocks in the way of a student of
American history.

The official decisions of the popes were for the most part set forth
in two forms of equal authority—Bulls and Briefs—and this was the

case whether the subject were a dogmatic deliverance upon a matter
of faith, a direction on a question of discipline, the creation or modification of an institution, or a decision in a secular matter as in the
present case. It is inaccurate to call these American Bulls "privileges
"issued in the particular form of the small Bulls, called by the ponti-
"fical chancery *tituli* or gracious acts."³ This is to confuse things
essentially different. A *privilege* in canon law is, by its very name,
a private or particular law, according a favour to some person or institution ; as, for instance, to a monastery or church " *Dicitur lex,*
" *non⁹ quia privilegium est lex, sed quia quamdiu duret instar legis*
" *observari debet: dicitur privata quia non facit jus quoad omnes.*" A
titulus is something still different, and is a presentation or right to a
benefice or a church. A privilege or title might, indeed, be in the
form of a Bull ; but whether the Bull was a small one or not, would
depend upon the bulk of the subject matter, and, on the other hand,
a small Bull might be of exceeding importance. The Bulls referred to
in this question are public laws ; international decisions involving an
inchoate right to half the world. They cannot be called "privileges,"
still less "titles ;" and to call them "small Bulls" in any sense is an
error, as the reader will see on reference to them in the appendix. A
still greater confusion is caused by Mr. Harrisse's explanation of the
word *litterae*. He says,¹⁰ in relation to the Bulls described later as A
and B, "The pontifical privileges were often accompanied by a second
" *littera*, shorter than the first, and of which it was, in fact, the noti-
"fication," and again referring to the Bull *Eximiae*, he says, ¹¹ "This
"*littera* was not exactly an abridgement of the primary Bull, resemb-
"ling, for instance, the abstracts of testaments, grants, bills of sale,
"or conveyances which our recorders deliver constantly." This is
very misleading, for the word *littera* is general and covers all written
communications. Nor is it correct to say that the " pontifical chan-
"cery drafted anew important Bulls in condensed form, which were
" transcribed in full in its registers, and were legalized not simply as
" true copies but as authentic originals."¹² That would be equivalent to
a legislature passing two acts covering the same subject, a long and a
short one, and making both original and authentic. Moreover, there
could be no "papal Bulls for common use"¹³ "carried round on maritime
"expeditions" to be shown while both the larger and "condensed orig-
"inals" were retained in the archives. This very singular error seems
to have been suggested by a clause in the Bull *Eximiae* as follows :

" But forasmuch as it would be very difficult for the present letters to be car-
' ried to all such places as may be expedient, we will," etc., etc., " that to copies
" of these presents, signed by a public notary, employed for that purpose and

" provided with the seal of some person endowed with ecclesiastical dignity, or
" with that of an ecclesiastical court, the same unquestioned faith shall be given,
" in a court of justice, or without, or anywhere else, as to these presents if they
" were shown or exhibited."

This clause is customary in Bulls or Briefs which are intended for wide circulation and will be found also in *Inter cetera*. It is so common that in some *Bullaria*, the first words alone are given "*Verum tamen difficile foret, etc., etc.*," with a note on the margin to the effect that " faith is to be given to copies." A clause almost in the same words occurs at the end of the encyclical of the present pope concerning the Jubilee which appeared in the newspapers a few months ago.

These two forms of expressing the decision of a pope vary in outward appearance. A Brief commences with an abridged formula. The name of the Pope is prefixed and the words, "*ad perpetuam rei memoriam*;" then it continues on with the main subject matter. It is written on paper, in a modern style of handwriting, dated according to the modern calendar and sealed in red wax with the "fisherman's ring."

A Bull, although it possesses no greater authority, is more formal in its salutation and more solemn ; as will be seen on reference to appendix A. "*Alexander, episcopus, servus servorum Dei, etc., etc.*" It is written on parchment and (until recently) was in an antique style of characters. It is dated according to the old Roman calendar : but the essential note is that the seal is of lead (it might be of gold) stamped on one side with the effigies of SS. Peter and Paul and, on the other, with the name of the reigning pope. The seal is attached by strings of various significant colours. There are other points of difference, but the above are the most striking.

It is of the essence of a law of any kind, and before all others of these pontifical laws which bind the conscience, that they shall be published or promulgated. A secret law is not a law in any sense of the word. Until it is promulgated it does not exist as a law and binds no one. It will be seen later how this fundamental principle has been entirely overlooked, and this is the more surprising, inasmuch as, by the laws of all Catholic countries in those days, every Bull, Brief or public letter of the popes had to be presented to certain royal officers and receive the royal *placet* or *exsequatur* before being published or even communicated to any other person whomsoever. The extract given on page 480 from a letter to his vice-roy by King Ferdinand the Catholic, will set this matter in a very clear light. In that way monarchs guarded their prerogatives ; for a Bull not promulgated in a country did not bind there. To get over this difficulty it was maintained by some

canonists that a Bull was sufficiently promulgated by being affixed to
the gates of the Vatican and proclaimed in the piazza of the[14] Campo di
Fiori at Rome. This was said to be publication *in urbe et orbi.* That
was disputed by others : but, without wandering into a disputed question, it may confidently be affirmed that a Bull unpublished and unknown to the persons whom it was intended to bind wanted that essential quality which brought it into life and force.

Now, while a Bull was in this inchoate state, it might be entered
on the secret register of the Vatican and might be complete in form ;
but, before promulgation, it was still open to modification. It might
be found on final examination that the instrument was not drawn in
precise accordance with the will or instructions of the Pope ; or some
omission or error might be pointed out by the person who had petitioned
for it. In such a case (and it is not at all an uncommon one) a new
Bull would be drafted and it also would be entered at its proper date
upon the register, while the first would never appear. This, as will be
shown, was what occurred in 1493, and recent researches having, after
three hundred and fifty years, unearthed the first draft, a controversy
has arisen most perplexing to students.

These documents, Bulls or Briefs, are known, and always cited by
the first words after the salutation. The present paper is chiefly concerned with two—the *Eximiae devotionis*, dated May 3, and the *Inter
cetera* dated May 4—both of 1493. It will at once be seen therefore
that it is paradoxical to write of two Bulls *Inter cetera* as issued on two
successive days of the same year covering the same subject matter. It
is like quoting two statutes on the same subject, of the same chapter,
of the same regnal year, identical in their wording, save in two or three
sentences. One of the chief objects of this paper is to clear up this
apparent difficulty. It has been brought forward very prominently of
late and magnified rather than explained.

IV.—THE DEMARCATION OF 1493.

On May 4, 1493, Pope Alexander VI. promulgated the Bull,
known from its first words as *Inter cetera*, in which he delimited, by a
line drawn from pole to pole, what would now be called the "spheres
"of influence" of Spain and Portugal. The Bull was sent to Spain by a
special messenger. It was received by the Catholic sovereigns and acted
upon. A copy was despatched to Columbus, then preparing for his
second voyage, and another to Fray Buil, who was going with him to
superintend the missions. It became the subject of innumerable discussions. Copies were made at the time and authenticated by ecclesi-

astical authority ; the original was deposited in the archives of the Indies at Seville where it remained until within very recent years ; it has been printed in all the *Bullaria:* referred to and cited in all the books. For three hundred years, no suspicion of any other *Inter cetera* arose in the minds of the numberless officials, annalists and historians, who administered American affairs or wrote on American subjects.

In the year 1797, Juan Baptista Munoz, who had been entrusted by the King of Spain with the task of writing a history of the New World, and to whom the archives of the kingdom had, for the first time, been thrown open, found, at Simancas, a document in the form of a Bull commencing with the same words *Inter cetera,* but dated May 3, (*quinto nonas Maii*) the day before the historic Bull, which bore date *quarto nonas Maii.* The two documents were, for the greater part of their contents, in identically the same words. In appendix A is printed the full text of the historic Bull of May 4, and all the words which are not in the Simancas document are printed in italics. On the other hand, all the words in the Simancas draft which were omitted in the Bull as promulgated are given in the footnotes, with references to the places from whence they were dropped. The reader has, therefore, practically both Bulls before him.

The discovery of the Simancas document gave rise to much speculation. Humboldt gave[15] a partial collation of the two Bulls and expressed surprise without offering an explanation. Washington Irving referred to both and did not attempt to reconcile them, but he gave the dates, erroneously, as May 2 and May 3 respectively. Munoz quoted the historical Bull containing the line, but he gave May 3 as the date. In his paper in the *American Historical Report,* Prof. Bourne gives a partial collation of the two, and Mr. Harrisse in his *Diplomatic History* has brought the difficulty into strong light, and has moreover increased it by treating the unpromulgated Bull as the primary one and as a valid and efficacious document. He calls it a "privilege," and says, "apparently within the twenty-four hours" after its publication, Alexander published the other. One of the chief objects of this paper is to show that the Simancas Bull, having never been published, never had the breath of legal life and also, by comparing the two documents, to explain the duplication by internal evidence.

The Bulls which Mr. Harrisse in his *Diplomatic History* brings under review, are four in number; he has lettered three of them as follows, for ready reference :

A. *Inter cetera* of May 3—the Simancas, unpublished Bull.

B. *Eximiae devotionis* of May 3.

C. *Inter cetera* of May 4—the promulgated Bull of
demarcation—the historic Bull.

And the fourth may be lettered D.

It is a Bull known only in a Spanish translation made sixty years
after its supposed date and entitled *Extension de la concesion y donacion
Apostolica de las Indias.*

These four documents, if all thrown together, are conflicting, but
a careful examination will eliminate A as an unpromulgated document
which never had a valid and legal existence, and show that D does not
affect the argument, in the first place, because no original copy has
ever been found or proved to have existed, and second, because, even
if it were a valid document, it adds nothing to the real Bull, being only
an explication of what had already been enacted. There will then
remain B and C, and these will be found, not only to harmonize, but
to supplement each other and to form, when taken together, a logically
consistent whole, such as the expert lawyers of the *Curia Romana*
would not be ashamed of.

While it may be held by extremists, in opposition to the great
majority of canonists, and the unanimous opinion of civil lawyers, that
a Bull, when affixed to the gate of the Vatican and proclaimed on the
piazza of the Campo di Fiori, was sufficiently promulgated to bind the
consciences of all Catholics, no one has yet ventured to assert that a Bull
never published at all, at Rome or anywhere else, had any efficacy
whatever. One well known instance there used to be of a Bull being
published annually in that way at Rome, because it was not admitted
to publication elsewhere in Europe ; but that was a very exceptional
case which proves the rule and the arguments from it have no validity
here, for this was a decision, not on dogma or discipline, but in a boundary
question, which Spain had applied for and, of necessity, it had to be
notified to the parties concerned who were fitting out expeditions and
extending discoveries into all seas. In this case, local publication was
of the very essence of the matter ; but the Simancas document lay unknown and unsuspected for three hundred years until Munoz found it
in 1797. It does not in the least validate the document to say that
when the present pope opened the archives of the Vatican, both Bulls
were found on the secret register of Alexander VI. There was, no
doubt, an intention to issue that dated May 3, but the entry of the
next day cancelled it and that without mention, because the first draft
was never uttered. In fact the very thing the Catholic sovereigns had
asked for, to wit, the line of demarcation, had been entirely lost sight
of and, therefore, the instrument was of necessity drafted anew. The
subject matter of the petition was then inserted and matter duplicated

in another Bull was omitted. The case is not parallel to that of the
preparation of dogmatic Bulls, but is parallel rather to a copy of the
judgment of some high civil court in which errors may be found on
examination before publication and the Spanish envoy on looking into
the first document could easily see that what his master had specially
asked for was not there.

With regard to the *Eximiae devotionis* (Mr. Harrisse's B) he is un-
doubtedly right in taking it to be a real Bull; but it is misleading to call
it a "privilege," and it is a *littera* in no other sense than other written
communications are *litterae*. The historians he refers to (without men-
tioning their names) who take the Bull to be "a simple invoice sent
"with Bulls A and C, when they were sent to Spain." must have wan-
dered from some shipping business into the regions of history and canon
law. Mr. Harrisse explains that it was not like an "invoice" or an
abstract of a "grant" or "testament" or "bill of sale" or "conveyance."
It was not "exactly an abridgment of the primary Bull ;" it might, he
thinks, be called "a papal Bull for common use." It certainly was very
far from being any one of these things. It was simply a deliverance
of the Roman court in the usual form of a Bull and, as will appear on
reading it in appendix B, it had a clear and distinct meaning, and the
sentence in it *"prout in nostris inde confectis litteris plenius continetur."*
refers to the line of demarcation intended to be in Bull A but omitted.
When the Bull was redrawn, the next day, as Bull C the clause omitted
was inserted, for that missing clause of demarcation was the essential
motive of the whole transaction. The Roman chancery was as Mr.
Harrisse observes evidently hurried beyond its usual leisurely pace.

The date of this Bull (B) is May 3—the same date as that of the
unpublished Bull. It is not met with in the ordinary books, and has
therefore, been given in appendix B. Mr. Harrisse has given it in an
English version. In appendix A of this paper is, as has been said, a
copy of Bull C—the historic Bull. If the reader will omit all the
words in italics and read into it all the words in the footnotes, in their
places as marked, he will reconstruct the text of the rejected draft.
He will see that the draughtsman erred in two directions, first, by making
mention of the rights of Portugal which were to form, and did form
the subject matter of a separate Bull (B) and, second, by omitting the
judgment of the Pope delimiting the territories of the two crowns.
The re-drafting of the Bull made the correction in both directions ;
for upon a careful comparison, it will appear that the matter dropped
from the first draft (Bull A) which is all shown in the footnotes in appendix A, refers solely to the rights of Portugal and is nothing else
than what is given in Bull B *Eximiae devotionis;* while the italicised

passages contain the inserted matter which was in effect the cardinal point of the whole movement. The two documents A and B, in fact overlap ; while the two documents B and C are supplementary and form a logical and consistent whole. The Bull C distinguishes the respective spheres of action of the two crowns, and the Bull B gathers up all the rights, which in previous Bulls had been conceded to Portugal in its sphere, and by one enactment without detailed recital, confers them upon Spain to be enjoyed solely in her own then definitely assigned sphere. In that way the two powers would be kept from coming into collision and the whole mass of prior legislation for Portugal, which extended over fifty years and was very voluminous, was enacted for Spain in a few sentences—by a device very common in drawing up legislation. This, Mr. Harrisse has not observed for he says, "apparently within the twenty-four hours which followed the publication " of the two Bulls, Alexander VI., May 4, published a third—Bull C." and then he proceeds to call it the second *Inter cetera*. This is underrating the Roman Chancery. Such blundering would not have passed in a village municipality ; for it was issuing two enactments of the same title and mainly in the same language within twenty-four hours. This Bull C is the only Bull of demarcation recorded in all the *Bullaria*, referred to in innumerable documents and the theme of numerous writers for three hundred years while what Mr. Harrisse calls the "primary Bull" mouldered unknown in the archives of Simancas.

In continuation of his remarks upon this Bull C, Mr. Harrisse says, "We know by the *Codex Diplomaticus* that there was attached to " that Bull a leaden seal fastened with silk strings, red and saffron " colour." Beyond doubt, for these as has been shown, are the marks of a genuine Bull and, in a Bull of grace, the seal is always attached with strings of coloured silk. Following the *Codex* further, we find that Peter Garcia, Bishop of Barcelona, on July 19, 1493, testified that he "had held, handled, seen and diligently examined these apostolic " letters of our most Holy Father and Lord in Christ, Alexander VI., " by Divine Providence Pope, from which hung his true Bull of lead " with threads of silk of a red and saffron colour, according to the style " of the Roman court, sound and entire in their marks, not vitiated, " nor erased, nor in any part suspicious, but free from any doubt what- " ever." Then he proceeds to give a copy of the Bull (as in appendix A). It was then at Barcelona and the Bishop had an official copy made and verified in the presence of certain named ecclesiastics and especially of an apostolic notary who was secretary of the Bishop of Seville. This copy was again collated with the original at Seville on Dec. 30, 1502, in the presence of witnesses. The whole is certified to by a

notary apostolic with formalities unnecessary to repeat. There can,
therefore, be no doubt as to which document is the "primary Bull."

If the Bulls B and C are considered together it will be seen that no
injustice was done to Portugal. The very mention of her rights *en bloc*
in the *Eximiae devotionis* and the grant of the same rights to Spain in
a different sphere confirmed them. Nothing was awarded to Spain,
but what she had discovered and what she might discover beyond a
certain line. The monarchs were not misled by the formal phrases
which scandalize modern writers as being "arrogant and presumptuous."
The decision is in the form of an absolute gift "We of our own motion,
" and not at your solicitation, nor upon petition presented in your name,"
when every one knew that the Bull was issued at the request of Spain.
In like manner in 1732, King George II. granted the charter of
Georgia to his petitioners, "of our special grace, certain knowledge,
" and mere motion," while the territory granted had been discovered
and was disputed by Spain. What the Pope really did was to confirm
each power in what it actually had and to allot "spheres of influence"
in which they might pursue their discoveries without quarrelling—pre-
cisely as an international congress might do at the present day. No
more account was taken of the Caribs and Indians than is taken now
of Africans, Philippinos, Chinese or Hawaiians. Of course, they get
the blessings of religion and civilization ; but those also were promised
in the Bulls and, in short, in view of recent movements towards a court
of international arbitration, the whole proceeding has a modern air—
there is as much fundamental justice in one case as in the other.

Finally there is a fourth document (see appendix C) which we have
lettered D. Mr. Harrisse states that it is "known at present only in a
" Spanish translation made Aug. 30, 1554, by one Gracian, doubtless
" Diego Gracian de Aldrete, then secretary of Philip II. for foreign
" languages." It is given in Navarrete as *Bula de la extension de la concesion y donacion apostolica de las Indias*. There is, indeed, a Latin
version in Solorzano, but Mr. Harrisse is doubtless correct in supposing
it to be a translation from the Spanish, necessary in a treatise written
in Latin. The most careful researches at Simancas, Seville and at
Rome, have failed to find any trace of an original of the Bull. Notwithstanding the frequency of forgeries of apostolical letters, said by
Mr. Harrisse to have existed in the time of Alexander VI., he thinks
that there was a valid original Bull. The letter cited by him does not
bear on the point. It was written by the Catholic sovereigns from
Barcelona, Sept. 5, to Columbus, then at Seville, preparing to start on
his second voyage. They wrote to ask his opinion on certain statements
made and say that, if they are true, the Bull (of May 4) should be

amended.   But the Bull D bears date Sept. 25, and twenty days is too
short a time to cover the transmission of a letter twice over the extreme
length of Spain and an application to Rome and the issue of a Bull based
upon it.   Munoz, Herrera, Humboldt and other authorities of weight in-
cidently notice this Bull without objecting to its authenticity, although
they had only the Spanish translation, and Mr. Harrisse is well supported
in his belief, not only by their authority, but by internal evidence; for this
Bull D is in effect nothing but such an interpretation or explication of the
Inter cetera as would likely have resulted from the persistency of
the extravagant claims of Portugal.   There is nothing in it to suggest
occasion for forgery.

Without raising the question of the existence of an original Bull, we
venture to think that Mr. Harrisse attaches to it a meaning which it
will not bear ; because, if it had been intended to cancel any of the
rights granted to Portugal in previous Bulls, that aspect would not have
failed to come to the surface in the negotiations which resulted in the
treaty of Tordesillas the following year, and, if Mr. Harrisse's contention
be right, it would have won the case for Spain without argument at the
Junta of Badajoz, but although the proceedings have been preserved
in great detail, this Bull was not alluded to.   The Roman court could
not, without cause assigned, revoke a decision in a secular matter made
to a great Catholic power.   No injustice was in fact done or attempted
to be done to Portugal, but Portugal was not allowed to strain the
meaning of the grants made to her so as to appropriate the discoveries
just made by Columbus for Spain.   These discoveries were supposed by
all to be in the "Indies."   The West and East Indies had not then
been separated in thought or name, nor was an intervening continent
then supposed to exist.   The Portuguese claimed that their Bulls .
covered the Indies, because their grant was "ad Indos," but they had
not then reached India by sea, though they had turned the Cape of
Good Hope.   The Spaniards had found some part, no one knew what,
of the Indies, and the Bull maintained them in their possession.   In
reading these old charters one must incessantly guard against the am-
biguity of the word East, because the American continent being non-
existent in their thoughts, they constantly spoke of reaching the East
on a westward course.

This Bull D, now under review, is supposed to bear date Sept.
25, 1493.   It commenced by saying that certain concessions had only
a short time before been made to Spain, referring to the Bulls B and C,
and then it confirmed them in all their clauses as fully as if recited
word by word—the line of demarcation, therefore, was confirmed in
the most absolute manner.   It stated that the grant had been made for

lands to the west and south and continued to the following effect (and here is the point of contention)—that since it may happen that, in sailing to the west and south, the Spanish sailors may discover land in eastern parts and lands which may belong to India, the Bulls of grant (B and C) are extended in all their clauses to cover such lands, whether they are or seem to be in the western, southern or eastern parts or in India. Then followed a *non obstantur* clause, evidently aimed at the excessive claims of Portugal, not revoking the Portuguese Bulls, but quashing the strained meaning put into them. The document then stated that, as by chance at some time or other, persons may have navigated these seas, nothing but actual and real previous possession was to avail in setting a bar to Spain in extending her discoveries on a western course. This principle of right by actual possession was adopted in the treaty of Tordesillas, and the reader will find in appendix D, Jaime Ferrer's opinion given to the Spanish monarchs that the Spanish demarcation might reach westwards round the world to the Arabian gulf, "*if our " ships go there first.*"

This view of the *Bula de la extension* is the one held by Navarrete. It is expressed as follows by Munoz, "to remove every doubt with re-" gard to those countries of the Indies to which the King of Portugal " might lay claim by virtue of former Bulls, the Holy Father declared " on the 26th of the following month of September, that all countries " of the Eastern Indies which the Spaniards might find in case they " were not already in Christian hands, should be included in the grant " made to the Catholic sovereigns." The principle laid down by the Pope was, as between the two powers, eminently just ; for Portugal was claiming by virtue of her Bulls, lands which none of her sailors had ever seen. The Pope swept away these pretensions and made his grant to follow discovery and possession. He drew no line in the East, and therefore the papal partition of the world is, as will be shown more fully—a popular myth. The reader will find this *Bula de la extension* in appendix C. It is given in the Latin version of Solorzano *De India- rum Jure*, Madrid, 1629.

V.—The First Line of Demarcation.

It was the opinion of Columbus and certainly, in 1493, no other opinion upon the subject was of equal weight, that on sailing westwards across a meridian about one hundred leagues west of the Azores, he had entered the New World, and he recorded in his journal that at that point the needles of all his compasses had crossed over from easterly variation to one point west of north. We cannot, at this day, realize the profound impression then made on the minds of that small company, alone on an unknown ocean where no keel had ever before sailed, when the compass, their sole hope for retracing their course, began, as they thought, to fail them. Curiosity and wonder filled the mind of the admiral and consternation the hearts of the men at crossing the threshold of a mysterious region where hidden and unknown forces commenced to operate. In a letter to the Catholic sovereigns, written in 1498, the admiral set forth his views as follows :—

"When I sailed from Spain to the Indies, I found that as soon as "I had passed a hundred leagues westward of the Azores, there was a "very great change in the sky and the stars, in the temperature of the "air and in the water of the sea : and I have been very diligent in ob- "serving these things. I remarked that from north to south, in travers- "ing these hundred leagues from the said islands, the needle of the com- "pass which hitherto had turned to the northeast, turned a full quarter "of the wind to the northwest, and this took place from the time we "reached that line."

He then went on to describe the Sargasso sea and other remark- able appearances which, under the tension of his first voyage, made an indelible impression upon his mind. Whether, in the light of our present knowledge, his views were correct or not, is beside the question. He held them to the last day of his life and we must take account of them.

With this fixed opinion Columbus returned from his first voyage and, driven by stress of weather into the Tagus, he went, in response to an invitation he dared not disobey, to visit the King of Portugal whom he found full of chagrin at the success of the expedition, as indeed he well might be, for, as every one then thought, the Indies, which in fifty, years of continuous effort the Portuguese had not reached, by the south and east around Africa, had been reached on a course almost directly to the west. In that interview Columbus learned that the King in- tended to lay claim to the whole of the supposed Indies and adjacent seas in virtue of Bulls issued at various dates from 1443 to 1484 as well as under existing treaties between the two kingdoms. This interview took place on March 10. The news went direct to Rome, then the centre of all intelligence, and reached there on April 11, before Colum- bus got to Barcelona to report in person to the Spanish sovereigns. He arrived at Palos on March 15, and from thence he sent an express to their Majesties with the news. He could not have failed to warn them of the claims made by the King of Portugal under the Papal Bulls, nor could he have failed to suggest so obvious a precaution as that of obtaining, at the earliest moment, a decision of the Pope to confirm Spain in the possession of the newly discovered lands. Con-

jecture amounts to certainty that Columbus indicated the line of one
hundred leagues west of the Azores as a natural and equitable boundary.
There was, as pointed out by Humboldt, a reasonable motive "for seek-
"ing to convert a physical into a political boundary line." He be-
lieved that lines of variation ran parallel to the meridians ; for on his
return from his second voyage, when the pilots, by reason of severe
storms, had lost their reckoning, he thought in that way to ascertain
his longitude. Mr. Harrisse is doubtless right in maintaining that
Portugal had no share in fixing the line of one hundred leagues. Fernan Columbus said that his father had suggested the line and everything
points that way. In the charter of privileges to the admiral the monarchs call it "the line which we have caused to be traced." The Spanish
envoys were instructed to inform the Pope that the discoveries had
been made without encroaching on the possessions confirmed to Portugal. In view of the existing treaty between the two crowns and the
Bulls granted at the instance of Portugal the request of Spain was
politic and reasonable and it was urged with promptness and vigour.

The line fixed by Alexander VI. was therefore a scientific line ;
based upon the very first observation ever made of magnetic variation,
and to cite Humboldt[16] again, " the Pope actually rendered, without
" knowing it, an essential service to nautical astronomy and the physical
" science of terrestrial magnetism." By directing attention to this new
fact he gave a stimulus to continued investigation. He was, therefore,
abreast with the latest physical discovery of his day, and he was ahead of
many, who during the Cabot discussions of the last few years, have been
tracing imaginary courses over the ocean while ignoring the prime factor
of terrestrial magnetism.

Upon careful reading there does not appear to be any vagueness
of language in the Bull. The Pope evidently distinguished between
what he knew and what he did not know. He stated the distance westward in leagues—a measure of length absolute in itself and familiar to
all mariners. He did not attempt to decide the circumference of the
earth or to fix the length of a degree. He and his officials had too keen
a sense of logic to regulate the length of a league, which was a known
and certain quantity, by the speculative length of a degree which was
an unknown and uncertain quantity. He did not, moreover, attempt
to fix the latitude and longitude of the Azores or Cape Verde Islands.
He was content to leave them wherever they might be and to measure
westwards in a definite direction with a definite measure from a definite
point—to wit, the most westward of either of the two groups of islands
in the Atlantic then held by right of discovery as possessions of
Portugal.

Nor was there any vagueness about the decision that the regions "westwards and southwards" of a line drawn from pole to pole should belong to Spain. Those words covered, and were meant to cover, a dangerous though unreasonable pretension of the King of Portugal made known to Columbus and made manifest in subsequent disputes—namely, that everything south of Cape Bojador whether west or east, belonged to Portugal. The words "westwards and southwards" cut that notion clearly out. Moreover the line was not to pass a hundred leagues west of the Azores and Cape Verde Islands as if they were on the same meridian. The Pope did not decide that, nor did he know whether or not all the islands of those groups had been discovered. The line was to be one hundred leagues westward of any one of the islands whatsoever of those two groups. Both groups were held by the King of Portugal—a Christian prince ; and a line one hundred leagues "*a qualibet insularum,*" as Eden translates, "from any of the islands," would be reasonable and allow a wide margin. The distance being westwards would commence to be measured from the most western of either of the groups.

The main object of the Bull *Inter cetera* was to turn the enterprises of the two nations in opposite directions by giving each a free scope east and west of the specified line, for as has been shown, the Bulls to Portugal were not revoked but confirmed by the *Eximiae devotionis.* For if the Pope had revoked these Bulls he could not have referred to them as specifically setting forth the powers he was granting to Spain in the regions discovered by her sailors. The grants to Portugal extended "*ad Indos,*" and the grant to Spain was "*versus Indiam*" —the expeditions of the former power were to be made east and south, and of the latter west and south ; one would reach India on the west side and the other on the east side. The Pope did not decide any line in the remote East, that was left to be settled by the principle that lands in the possession of any Christian prince were excepted from the scope of the Bull. That point did not become practical until Magellan's expedition reached the Philippine Islands and El Cano brought home the news. Meantime, in 1493, Portugal was chiefly concerned to get more extended limits upon the Atlantic, because, for aught any one then knew, some great southern continent might exist, such as Pomponius Mela had indicated, and of that Portugal wanted to have as large a share as possible. The principle is the same as that of the line of the treaty of Tordesillas laid down in the following year (1494) which was in effect (see appendix D) that the Catholic monarchs might claim anything discovered in sailing to the East on a westward course even as far as Arabia—*if only the Spanish ships arrived there first.*

The foregoing is an attempt to read the Bull in the light of its own time. It was the last of its kind and marked the close of an era ; for the great revolt against Rome was rapidly approaching and the storm was soon to break. The Bull bound Spain and Portugal, as regards each other, for they were parties to such references. As to how far it might be held by canon law to bind other nations is not necessary here to inquire. Henry VII. did not hesitate to send Cabot west of the line, and Francis I. sent Verazzano, and England and France founded claims to parts of America upon their voyages ; but, however that may be, the treaty of Tordesillas in 1494, abrogated the line established by the Pope and laid down another and this last line, and not Pope Alexander's line, is the one spoken of in the books as the " line of " demarcation ;" it is not the papal line at all, and although, in A.D. 1506, it was confirmed by Pope Julius II., it had been drawn by Spain and Portugal as if they alone had any concern with the matter. It will be of interest to state here that there has been found in the secret archives of the Vatican a document entitled " De Canadia et Nova " Francia," setting forth an elaborate argument that the Pope's decision did not apply to the discoveries of Verazzano, because the grant was limited by its express words to "islands and mainlands," " per " nuncios et capitaneos vestros inventae" i.e., discovered by Spanish ships. The argument is ingenious, but it is also sound and applies as well and with more force to the voyages of the Cabots. The Papal line of demarcation was a terminus a quo—no terminus ad quem was fixed. The fact of discovery was to fix the latter, for the grant to Spain would travel eastwards with every discovery until her sailors came to lands in the possession of some Christian prince. There can be no doubt upon this point if the Bulls are carefully read—the westward progress of Spain was to be limited only by the eastward progress of Portugal. Mr. Harrisse is correct in writing of the "alleged" partition of the globe by Pope Alexander. The globe got divided somehow in the diplomacy between Spain and Portugal. It was a lay arrangement. The Pope drew a line on the Atlantic and gave the two nations a fair start, as it were back to back. As for the far East it was only the assumption of the disappointed kings of Portugal that the popes had granted to them unknown and undiscovered lands. The Bull awarded territories, when they were discovered in certain specified directions, upon the condition that when they were discovered they were also found unoccupied by any Christian prince.

VI.—The Treaty of Tordesillas in 1494.

Up to the year 1491 the Portuguese had made no discoveries beyond the Cape of Good Hope. In seventy years of continued effort along the coast of Africa they had succeeded in reaching the turning point towards the east and south of Asia. It was not until 1497 that Vasco de Gama led the way to India by sea—up to 1494 all the discoveries had been southwards. Successive popes had, upon solicitation, confirmed these discoveries and had also adjudged to Portugal the seas and lands discovered or to be discovered from Cape Bojador southward and eastward as far as the Indies, *"usque ad Indos."* Spain had admitted these claims by treaty in 1479, and had bound herself to refrain from interference. Portugal, in the meantime, had sent agents overland to Arabia and India who had reported upon the wealth of these regions, and was preparing with confidence to open up the eastern trade when the return of Columbus from his first voyage dissipated her dreams of monopoly : for he was supposed to have touched the eastern shore of the long coveted land of spices. It was a bitter disappointment to the King and he at once laid claim to more than the Bulls or the treaty would warrant. Columbus in the interview at Valparaiso assured King John that he had strictly followed the orders of his sovereigns and had avoided the regions conceded to Portugal, and the same statement was made at Rome when Spain applied for a Bull of confirmation. It was made with truth : for, whatever theories a few scholars may have held, no one before Columbus seriously attempted to go to the Indies by the west, and all the Bulls, as well as the treaty, had been drawn solely in contemplation of voyages by the south and east.

The objective point of both nations still lay open to further discoveries, though from opposite directions, for neither *"usque ad Indos"* or *"versus Indiam,"* carried an inclusive grant of the coveted regions to either party. As Mr. Harrisse properly points out, the Pope had not concerned himself with the other side of the world in laying down his line of demarcation ; but it was, in fact, left to be decided by discovery. With commendable desire to avoid war the two nations entered into negotiation, and the first proposition of Portugal was that the line should run east and west along the parallel of latitude of the Canary Islands, and that the activities of Spain should be confined to the regions north of that line. This was to attribute to the word "southward" of the Portuguese Bulls an absolute meaning that it would not bear. An attempt was also made to strain the meaning of *"usque ad Indos,"* and make it cover the Indies whose eastern margin Columbus was supposed to have touched. It is especially to be observed here that if the supposed *Bula de la extension y donacion* of Sept. 25, 1493, had possessed the meaning attributed to it by Mr. Harrisse and others, it would have obviated discussion : for the regions in dispute would have been conceded to Spain. From the fact that no such Bull was alluded to in the tedious preliminary discussions, we may fairly argue that either there was no such Bull or that it had no meaning beyond that attributed to it in the previous chapter.

Three envoys from each nation met at Tordesillas, and on June 7, 1494, signed the famous treaty which during three hundred years was a subject of dispute ; first, in the East, with reference to the Moluccas, and then in the West, with reference to the boundary between Brazil and the Spanish provinces in South America. The result was that without mention of any Bulls a line of demarcation was fixed much further westwards. But it was not 270 leagues farther west, as often stated, for the line of the Pope was a hundred leagues west of the Azores, and the line of the treaty was 370 leagues west of the Cape Verde Islands, so that the six degrees of longitude between these two groups must be deducted from the apparent additional extension. The treaty was confirmed twelve years later by Pope Julius II., on January 24, 1506. Then the treaty line was legally substituted for the line of Alexander VI.; though, in fact, no other line than the treaty line has been found on any map : even on those made as early as 1501-2. It will therefore be seen that the division of the world into two parts was a development of the treaty of Tordesillas, and that this "arrogant pre-" sumption"—the cause of so much indignant writing—is not properly laid to the charge of Pope Alexander.

Much of the literature on this subject would lead the general reader to suppose that the Bulls of concession to Spain and Portugal were a mass of pretentious and contradictory documents issued from time to time on no settled plan. On the contrary they will be found consistent with each other throughout the series, and from the first to the last, the principle of a primary right by discovery is a key to their true interpretation. They are sometimes diffuse as are the legal documents of other courts on account of the technicalities with which they are drawn. It is misleading to associate with them the least notion of infallibility, as if they touched upon any question of faith or morals. They were in fact decisions of a court of appeal. Every one of them was issued upon a petition by one power or the other—there were only two nations then engaged in discovery—and the rights of both were considered with care. The last of the series, that of Leo X., Nov. 3, 1514, in reaffirming all the grants to Portugal, did not imply that these rights had been abrogated. The change in the location of the line had been homologated by Julius II, and that remained as established by the treaty. It has remained. as appears in the first part of this paper. to be cited in the Venezuelan argument, and Mr. Bourne is in error in supposing that it was abrogated by the Bull of Leo X. and the right by discovery substituted then. The right by discovery and occupation is an inheritance from the Roman civil law and existed all the while. It was the real law running under all the Bulls. The form of donation was transitory and superficial.

The line of the treaty was an arbitrary line, based on no attempt at a rational or scientific principle. It was a mere compromise and it is worthy of remark that Columbus, in the deed of entail made at Seville (Feb. 21, 1498), as well as in his last will, ignored the treaty and cited the line of the Bull in its own terms. There was a stipulation in the treaty that within ten months a joint expedition should measure off these leagues of western extension, from the Cape Verde Islands to the dividing line, and if land were found the line was to be marked by a tower or pyramid. That expedition never sailed. The coast of America was soon recognized as a bar to the Eastern Indies and the Portuguese pressed on their discoveries and conquests to the farthest East, relieved from the apprehension of interference from Spain.

The return of El Cano, Magellan's lieutenant, in 1521, by way of the Cape of Good Hope, again awakened the Portuguese from their dreams of monopoly and showed them that their success in shifting the line westwards on the Atlantic was likely to lose them the Spice Islands (Moluccas) in the Pacific. How the idea of continuing the line round the globe first arose does not clearly appear. It was not in the Bull nor is it expressly in the treaty ; but in the negotiations which arose immediately upon the return of El Cano, it was taken for granted by all as if it existed by necessary implication in both documents while in fact no *terminus ad quem* can be found in either.

Collisions between the Spanish and Portuguese in the far East began to grow sharp and threatened to bring on war when a convention, known as the "Junta of Badajoz." assembled at that city on April 11. 1524, to decide upon the partition of the world between the two powers. for no others were considered in the matter. Sebastian Cabot was there as an expert pilot for Spain. He could have told them, and perhaps did tell them, that the flag of England had been already planted on the coast of the western continent. If he did tell them of Baccallaos. no record remains of it. Fernan Columbus was there also, and El Cano and Stephen Gomez, and Nuno Garcia, and Diego Ribeiro.

all as naval assessors for Spain. Portugal also sent pilots, amongst them some who had sailed in the East. It will be necessary to revert again to this convention : the point to be noticed here is that the pilots and sailors and astronomers were assessors to give professional information and that there were really two separate processes or inquiries. One related to the location of the line of demarcation, the other to the facts of prior possession or discovery. The Moluccas were the chief subject of dispute and while the Spaniards claimed that they had discovered them, without sailing over Portuguese waters, the Portuguese insisted that they had been there first. It is, therefore, evident that the doctrine of right by discovery was strongly held by both sides. The argumentation is very modern in its method. The Emperor insisted that, even if Portugal had discovered the islands (which he denied), that it would not give a title without possession taken, and that no one could truly say that he had found anything which he had not taken possession of. This is the precise statement of law in the British case against Venezuela (p. 150). " that it is not the finding of a thing but the taking " by the finder that gives the title," so that here we have the Emperor Charles V. anticipating Grotius by a hundred years, and Bluntschli and the British foreign office by four hundred years, in a most important doctrine of international law ; and the Emperor went on to appeal to the principles of "general law and natural reason." We may, therefore, see that the only new principle in this branch of international law is a definition of "possession" in a stricter sense, made as late as 1888 at Berlin. The Badajoz Junta was without result. The Portuguese would do nothing but assert that the islands were theirs and call upon Spain to give them up first and then try to prove the contrary, while the Spaniards maintained that they had the islands by possession, but would give them up if Portugal would establish her right by an action under the stipulations of the treaty.

In 1680, disputes arose about the treaty line on the other side of the world—on the River Plate in South America—and another convention met, with no better result. The matter was settled in 1750, not by reason or law, but in consequence of a marriage between the two royal houses.

It remains now to observe that the only rational line drawn on the ocean was that drawn by Pope Alexander VI., and that his line was almost immediately superseded by another, decided upon by the only two nations seriously occupied at that period in making discoveries. The new line was drawn without reference to the Pope and although during the past four hundred years the papal line of demarcation has been the theme of much indignant writing, the Spaniards and Portuguese were

all that time disputing about another line—one of their own making.
Last of all when, in 1885, the present Pope arbitrated upon the dispute
concerning the Caroline islands, situated near the western edge of the
grant supposed to have been made by his predecessors, he made not
the least reference to that, but decided consistently with his predecessors according to the underlying principle of law.

VII.—THE POINT OF DEPARTURE.

The commissioners at Tordesillas made no improvement on the Bull
of Pope Alexander in point of clearness ; for their distance of three
hundred and seventy leagues was made to commence from the Cape
Verde Islands generally, and that group extends over three degrees of
longitude. These islands are distant about 320 miles from Cape Verde
in Africa. They are barren and when discovered by the Portuguese
in A.D. 1456, were uninhabited. They were of considerable importance while the Portuguese were extending their discoveries southwards
along the coast of Africa and, in the old narratives of voyages, they are
often mentioned.

At first, while the islands of the West Indies were supposed to be
outlying portions of the East Indian archipelago, and still more, after
A.D. 1500, when Cabral discovered Brazil, the Portuguese claimed the
most western island of the group, San Antonio, as the initial point for
the western measurement. In that way the western limit of their demarcation area was made to include a greater stretch of the continent
now known as South America. The Spaniards were not so certain
about it, however, and in A.D. 1495, the Spanish sovereigns consulted
Don Jaime Ferrer on the meaning of the treaty and he gave his opinion
that Fogo, the central island, should be the point of departure. His
opinion is still extant in full, and may be found in Navarrete. Vol. II.
A translation is appended (Appendix D) and is worth careful perusal,
The question submitted was chiefly in regard to some practical method
of measuring the 370 leagues upon the Atlantic ocean ; but incidentally,
it becomes clear that Ferrer, in 1495, had no idea that the Pope, or
anybody else, had made a partition of the world ; for he says that the
eastern lands "on the Arabian Gulf side will belong to the sovereigns,
" our masters, should their vessels first navigate there." This single
sentence demonstrates beyond cavil that Pope Alexander had not
attempted to divide the world ; and that the doctrine of right by discovery was the prevailing doctrine of international law then, as now.
It also indicates that the development of the idea of a partition line in
the far East had not, up to 1495, set in.

Two years later, A.D. 1497, Vasco de Gama led the first Portuguese expedition to India and, following in his track, a swarm of adventurous sailors and soldiers very quickly opened up all the eastern regions. India, China, Siam, Malacca, Java, Borneo, Sumatra and the archipelago of islands were visited to an unknown extent; for the Portuguese were very reticent and made it a capital offence to communicate to foreigners a map of their discoveries in the East. Still, the news of the wonderful riches of those lands spread over western Europe. The ships returned with cargoes, and successful captains made establishments, and successful sailors brought home marvellous tales. From all this Spain was excluded ; for on the west, to the north and south, stretched the interminable barrier of America, and all search for an opening through it had been in vain. Secure in her monopoly Portugal was therefore anxious only to stretch her demarcation area westward over Brazil.

Among the Portuguese adventurers who had returned from the farthest East was Ferdinand Magellan—the greatest sailor of those days. In resentment for personal affronts he renounced his allegiance and passed over to Spain. His knowledge and experience led a Spanish expedition through the strait, which still bears his name, and across the great South Sea to the coveted Spice Islands in the East. In 1521, one of his captains, Sebastian El Cano, returned by way of the Cape of Good Hope. The world had been circumnavigated—the farthest East had been reached by sailing on a western course, and for the second time, the Portuguese hope of a monopoly of eastern trade was shattered.

We have seen in our enlightened age the United States on the brink of war with Great Britain because they supposed the latter held against a Spanish power an inconceivably minute and valueless portion of one half of what was in dispute in 1521. But Spain and Portugal did not go to war in 1521 ; although their people were kindred in speech. They resorted to negotiation instead. It is very remarkable that there was no blustering. Perhaps it was the absence of newspapers—perhaps it was the want of free representative institutions; it is sufficient to say that the convention, called the Junta of Badajoz, met in 1524, as explained in previous pages, and endeavoured to settle the question.

The Portuguese then saw their error in shifting westward the Pope's line of demarcation ; for the principle of prolonging the line of Tordesillas round the globe had become established and the further west the line was placed upon the Atlantic, the greater would be the extent of territory in the far East to be brought within the Spanish

sphere of influence. The Portuguese envoys shifted their ground at
Badajoz and claimed the most eastern islands of the Cape Verde group
as the proper point of departure : hoping thus to gain the Spice Islands
in the East. They took their stand upon the stipulation that the expedition, contemplated in the treaty of Tordesillas, was to assemble at
the Canaries, and from thence. proceed to the Cape Verde Islands to
commence the westward measurement. The islands, they argued, being mentioned in the plural, were to be taken as a group, and Sal and
Bonavista (written Boavista) the most eastern islands were the most important. We have, in British America, an interest in two islands of
this group for two localities on the east coast of Newfoundland—Fogo
and Bonavista—were from the earliest days named after them. But
without stopping to discuss that fact we find the Portuguese envoys,
in 1524, insisting on Bonavista being the proper point of western departure. The Portuguese contention was by no means well founded,
because these two eastern islands are the smallest of the group and do
not contain four per cent of the population. The Spanish envoys con-
tended for San Antonio—the most western point—and, although their
main motive was to bring the Spice Islands within their line, they had
the better argument, for San Antonio is the second in size and in population. The Portuguese protracted the negotiations and, as they
thought to gain more by delay, they made difficulties until the conference separated without arriving at a decision. As a matter of fact,
ascertained many years later when accurate estimation of longitude
could be made, the Spice Islands and Philippines did fall within the
Spanish demarcation. One hundred years later a dispute arose about
territory on the Rio de la Plata, and the two nations again exchanged
bases ; for Portugal argued for San Antonio and Spain for Bonavista.
It may therefore be safely concluded that Pope Alexander VI. and the
Roman Curia were better geographers and international lawyers than
the political envoys, either at Tordesillas or Badajoz.

VIII.—Ancient and Mediæval Measures of Length.[17]

At first sight nothing could appear more easy than to determine
the line of demarcation fixed by the treaty of Tordesillas. A locality
from whence to start, a definite direction in which to sail, and a definite
distance to be attained, were all specified, apparently, plainly enough ;
nevertheless it has been the subject of interminable disputes and recently in the Venezuelan dispute when the question was supposed to
have become academic, it once more came to the surface of practical
political debate.

To the statesmen of the sixteenth century the ownership of the Moluccas and the western limit of Brazil depended upon the solution of this question. To sailors and scholars it involved the great riddle of the age, "the secret of longitude:" for on the unquiet ocean, these leagues of Tordesillas could not be measured, nor marked, save by astronomical methods requiring a knowledge of the length of a great circle of the earth and consequently of the length of a degree of the equator.

Now, so far as the absolute distance is concerned, to wit, the three hundred and seventy leagues of the treaty, the circumference of the earth had no more to do with it than the circumference of the moon. The difficulty was solely in the practical measurement of distances at sea which the necessity of the case required to be resolved into degrees of longitude. The only method then known was by dead reckoning, and the deceptive character of that mode is manifest in the simple fact that, at the convention of Badajoz in 1524, the maps shown differed by forty-six degrees. We now know, within a few miles, the circumference of the earth and all are agreed as to the length of a degree, but so hard is it to realize the difficulties of past ages that many writers, down to even recent periods, have transposed and applied to marine leagues, the uncertainties which really existed with regard to degrees only. This is confusing to the student, for all the old navigators reckoned in leagues and whether we are following the journals of Columbus, or Cartier, or Champlain, it is necessary, if we wish to be exact, to have clear notions concerning this general standard of sea distances. By unguarded language on this subject, Mr. Harrisse is entangling our early history anew ; for in his *Diplomatic History,* he writes of *leagues* of Enciso, *leagues* of Ferrer, *leagues* of Columbus, as if they differed in length, instead of writing of *degrees* of Enciso, of Ferrer, of Columbus ; for, while the leagues were the same, the degrees differed in the number of leagues they contained, and when Mr. Harrisse takes varying and erroneous quantities and makes them perform trigonometrical functions, the confusion is made worse ; since the sine, cosine, tangent or square of an erroneous quantity acquires no value from being found in mathematical tables—rather the contrary, because to square a mistake is to raise it to a higher power of error.

It is beyond the scope of this paper to discuss the numerous national and provincial land leagues or miles. The inquiry will be confined to the marine league of Columbus and other sailors during the period of the great expansion of European nautical enterprise. For ready reference, it is convenient here to remind the reader that the circumference of the earth is now taken to be 21,600 nautical or geographical miles. In statute miles it is variously calculated from 24,874 to 25,020 miles, for, as the earth is not a perfect sphere, these measurements are only close approximations. For the same reason, the length of a degree on the equator is estimates at from 69·1 to 69·5 statute miles. In current speech the latter measure is sometimes given, though the former is more nearly correct.

All the countries of Western Europe which fell under the influence of Rome retained permanent traces of the itinerary measures of the Empire in the mile, or *mille passuum* of the Roman soldier. In the Latin countries the measure persisted ; and even in England, nearly until the end of the reign of Elizabeth, the mile was 5000 feet or 1000 paces ; and was only 146 feet longer than the Roman mile. In the eastern part of the Empire the Greek stadium was the standard and so continued until the Mohammedan invasion. The Roman geographers borrowed their science from the Greeks and used in their writings the Greek standard measure, and this continued to be the measure used by writers on cosmography throughout the middle ages : for after the time of Ptolemy no original work was done, save by the Arabians, until long after the period now under review. The stade is continually cited in the literature of the age of Columbus and it is a very convenient measure, for it bore an accepted and simple ratio to the mile and league of those days. Ptolemy was the chief authority, but the works of Aristotle. Eratosthenes, Strabo and other Greeks, as well as the Roman writers. Pliny. Macrobius and Pomponius Mela. were continually referred to with deference. It is difficult to realize the persistent weight of the authority of Ptolemy. Not until 1569 did Gerard Mercator lead the way in revolt and all traces of the great error of Ptolemy, as to the length of the Mediterranean Sea, did not disappear from the maps until the beginning of the last century. For 1500 years Ptolemy reigned supreme and, therefore, it is not lost labour to study the Greek geographers. if we wish to understand the age of Columbus.

The true circumference of the earth was not known to the Greeks, and they made different estimates : from Aristotle. 400.000 stades, to Ptolemy, 180,000 stades. The estimated length of a degree of the equator varied in proportion, from 1111 $^1|_9$ to 500 stades respectively. In Appendix E. I have given a comparative table of the length of the equator and of a degree thereof as held by the chief geographical writers, from Aristotle down to the date of the convention at Badajoz. The figures are given in Greek stades, and Italian leagues and miles. In a separate column is the translation of these figures into nautical miles of the present day. The compilation has been made in order to assist the student in grasping quickly the value of these ancient measures.

Putting aside Aristotle and Archimedes, they fall into three schools—those who follow Eratosthenes and reckon 700, those who follow Ptolemy and reckon 500 stades to a degree, and those who follow the Arabian measurements. The true length of a degree is 600 stades ; so that one school erred by one hundred stades in excess and another by 100 stades in defect. Lelewel states very confidently that Pytheas of Marseilles estimated the degree at 600 stades ; thus making the circumference of the earth 216,000 stades ; the precise equivalent of our 21,600 nautical miles. This, if true, would be exceedingly interesting ; but after examining Lelewel's authorities, I have not ventured to include Pytheas in the table.

The science of the Greeks loomed very large to the eyes of the cosmographers of the fourteenth and fifteenth centuries, and they entertained the opinion that the Greeks knew the true circumference of the earth and that if the great geographers of antiquity differed in the number of stades at which they estimated it, the difference was caused by their use of stades of various lengths. There was nothing in the Greek writings to suggest any such opinion. The Greek authors used the word "stades" without any qualification and without any apparent fear of being misunderstood : plainly intending in all their arguments, the Olympic stade of 600 Greek feet, which was the length of the foot-race course at the Olympic games. In the third century of our era, after the work of the geographers was over, there did come into use, in Egypt and in the Asiatic provinces of Rome, a stade of which seven and a half went to the Roman mile. This stade, called the Phileterian stade, affected the measures of the Arabs and its influence appeared in the writings of Alfragan and passed thence into the works of Bacon and D'Ailly and, through them, into the speculations of Columbus.

The idea of different stades having been used by the Greek cosmographers is first met with, says Humboldt, in a memoir by Jaime Ferrer to the Spanish sovereigns relative to the line of demarcation. This is an exceedingly interesting document and, as it throws strong light upon the nautical science of the period in review, a translation is given at Appendix D. Ferrer said that the 252,000 stades of Eratosthenes, the 180,000 of Ptolemy and the measurements of Strabo, Alfragan and Macrobius were the same in sum : but that the stades of Ptolemy were larger. (See App. D). Ptolemy, at that time, was an authority not to be gainsaid and yet Ferrer held, with Eratosthenes, that in a degree of a great circle, there were 700 stades of eight to a Roman mile. This heroic method of reconciling the ancient authors gained ground in an uncritical age and was advocated later by Delisle, Freret, Gosselin and many others, down to the early years of the present

century. Under the influence of this perennial fountain of error the
subject became an arena of confusion. Without wearying the reader
by going over this maze of unsettled opinion it will be sufficient to
refer to the pages of Lelewel; for although, in his work on Pytheas,
he distinguishes only two kinds of stades, the Olympic of eight to a mile
and the Italic of eight and one third to a mile, in his larger work there
are bewildering dissertations on the different stades and miles of ancient
authors. We read of very small stades 10 or $12\frac{1}{2}$ to a mile, of Phileterian stades $7\frac{1}{2}$ to a mile which later became 7 to a mile, of stades 5 to
a mile, of Posidonian stades 500 to a degree, of stades of latitude, and
of stades 502 $^1\!/_2$ to a degree. Then we may read of miles of longitude,
of Venetian miles 60 to a degree, of miles 80 and 85 to a degree. In
one map he finds seven different valuations of miles—50, 55, 67, 83,
86 and 90 to a degree, and he naively remarks that this inequality of
miles to a degree is common to nearly all the maps of the middle ages.
Thus the absurdity is plainly apparent of taking these maps as seriously
as if they had been compiled by scientific survey, and of making
measures in common and daily use, such as the stade and the mile,
shift and vary proportionately to the errors on the early maps and to
suit the speculative notions of men groping during 2000 years to discover the true circumference of the earth and the corresponding length
of a degree of longitude. These "fancy stades," as D'Avezac called
them, are "will o' the wisp" lights to beguile the student of historical
geography.

The researches of Colonel Leake cleared away this fog and his
views were supported by Uckert, Muller, St. Martin and later writers
so that it may be now be considered as established that the stade of the
Greek writers was equivalent to 600 Greek feet, equal to 606·75 English
feet. From this arises a convenient and very nearly accurate ratio for
converting, at sight, the Greek stades into our own familiar nautical
miles, as follows :—

$$
\begin{array}{llll}
\text{1 Olympic stade} & = 606{\cdot}75 & \text{English feet.} \\
\text{10} \quad '' \quad\quad '' & = 6067{\cdot}5 & '' & '' \\
\text{and} \\
\text{1 nautical mile} & = 6075{\cdot}5 & '' & '' \\
\text{1 admiralty knot} & = 6086{\cdot}5 & '' & '' \\
\text{or by Clarke's measurement} & = 6087{\cdot}11 & '' & ''
\end{array}
$$

Therefore 10 Olympic stades = 1 minute of the equator,
and   600   ''   '' = 1 degree   ''   ''

The Greek and modern standards then, though not absolutely
equivalent, are sufficiently so for all practical purposes. The difference
between ten Greek stadia and our accepted nautical mile is not greater
than that between the nautical mile of customary computation and the

admiralty knot: and, as before stated, the precise circumference of the earth has not even yet been ascertained with absolute accuracy.

Although the Greek itinerary standard was the stadium, or foot-race course at Olympia, it was repeated in the stadia of all other Greek cities in Europe or Asia Minor, erected for the athletic games, of which the Greeks were so fond : and, in fact, wherever Greek influence extended the stade continued to be the established standard.

The Roman standard itinerary measure was characteristic of the world-conquerors. The mile is the *mille passuum*—the thousand paces—of the legionary soldiers, and, as they subdued Western Europe, the Roman power was consolidated by a perfect system of roads, and their milestones recorded the distances and familiarized the people for many centuries with a general standard of length which overrode the local measures of the shifting and semi-barbarous tribes of the West. The integer of this standard is the *passus*—the pace : not the *gradus*, or step—a distinction sometimes overlooked : because, as the word passed through the French into the English language it became synonymous with step : whereas the Roman *passus* was a double step equal to five Roman feet. In the British army the step is two and a half feet and the *passus* is five feet : but the Roman soldier had a slightly shorter step and his thousand paces were equivalent to only 4,854 English feet. I am not forgetting that, along the Rhine, there existed in the army, in the later years of the Empire, a longer foot—the Drusian foot—equal to 13·1 English inches : but the standard in law and the measure along the roads was the Roman mile, related to the Roman foot of 11·65 English inches. The following is a short table of these standards :

    1 Roman mile   = 1000 passus = 4854 English feet.
    1 Old English mile = 1000 paces = 5000   "   "
    1 modern statute mile   = 5280   "   "
    75 Roman miles (75·09)   = 1 degree.

It is instructive to observe that even the old English mile is based upon the idea of a thousand paces. "Our ancestors," as Professor De Morgan remarked, "if they had not the old Roman mile, thought they "had it." The difference was only 146 feet ; for the Roman foot being 11·65 English inches, 63 Roman are equivalent to 61 English feet. Capt. John Davis, of Arctic fame, one of the most skilful sailors of Queen Elizabeth's reign gives in his *Seaman's Secrets* (a treatise on navigation published in 1595) the following table : — 10 inches = 1 foot ; 5 feet = 1 pace ; 1000 paces = 1 mile; 3 miles = 1 league ; 20 leagues = 1 degree. The editor of *Davis's Works* in the *Hakluyt Series* adds a note to say that this must be misprint as a mile is 5,280 feet : but it is no misprint but an accurate statement of measures then in common use.

The expression *statute mile* suggests the existence of an older customary mile but. while the shorter measures are often mentioned in the statutes of the early parliaments. they make no references to miles, nor do they define a mile in any way.   Our *statute mile* first made its appearance in 35 Eliz. cap. vi. a statute making certain regulations concerning building houses within three miles of London.   Incidentally to its object and. as if some necessity existed for the definition. the mile intended is said to consist of eight furlongs.   The mile of 5000 feet contains only 7½ furlongs, 3 perches and 2 palms ; but the new mile is divisible into 8 furlongs, into 320 perches, poles or rods, and into 1760 yards : which native English measures, while they form convenient divisors of the statute mile of 5280 feet, cannot be harmonized with the Roman mile of 5000 feet.

If. then. the Roman mile persisted in England down to the last year of the reign of Elizabeth. with only the slight modification above noted. there is little cause for wonder that it should have persisted in its integrity in the countries round the Mediterranean where the Romance languages are spoken : and these were the countries wherein the great navigators were born and from which issued the expeditions of early discovery to the East and West Indies.   Cabot and Verazzano were Italians, in the service of England and France respectively. and their voyages were the foundations of the claims of these nations in North America.   The earliest literature of marine adventure is in Spanish, Portuguese, Italian and Latin, and the integer of distance is, throughout, the Roman mile known as the Italian mile and its multiple the Italian league—the marine league of the Mediterranean.

The student of the early narratives meets continually with the league as a measure common to all.   Whether it be Columbus, Vespucci, Magellan, Cabot, Diaz, De Gama, Galvano, Cartier, Ramusio or Oviedo, it is always the marine league in which their distances are calculated and Hakluyt in his translations carried them over without explanation, qualification or change.   Sometimes we meet with miles, but they are the Italian or Roman miles.   I am leaving out of the question the Swiss, Danish and German miles and leagues, because these nations took no part in early discovery and did not fall under the Roman power; but among the great maritime nations of Europe during the period under review, the marine league was a standard as universal as was the stade in Greek civilization and Greek geography.

The word league (Low Latin leuca and leuga) is Celtic and signifies a stone, in some Celtic tongues a flat stone, and was probably a road mark.   It was a measure used in Celtic Gaul in the time of Ammianus Marcellinus and seems to have been originally 1500 *passus* in length.

It was in use, in early times, by the sailors of the Mediterranean, as a
sea measure exactly equivalent to four Roman or Italian miles. The
writers of the period of expansion had, therefore, no need to qualify or
translate their nautical distances, for they were understood by all, at the
simple ratio of eight stades to a mile and four miles to a league. Notions
concerning "fancy stades" and "fancy leagues" are anachronistic stumbling blocks in the way of a student. The early writers did indeed
speculate much as to how many leagues went to a degree ; but not as
to the length of a stade, a mile or a league. These latter were their
standards, in which they were trying to work out the length of a great
circle of the earth and of its three hundred and sixtieth part, to wit,—
a degree. They were the known elements— the a and b of the problem;
the length of a degree was the x and y—the unknown quantity. The
league was an absolute measure—any man might pace it off on any road
—the degree depended upon the circumference of the earth, and it is
evident that the 370 leagues of the treaty of Tordesillas would extend
to a far greater western longitude on the shrunken globe of Columbus
than on the expanded globe of Jaime Ferrer's imagination.

As "fancy stades" of 1111 $\frac{1}{9}$, 833 $\frac{1}{3}$, 700 and 500 to a degree were
invented by geographers, from Don Jaime Ferrer down to recent times,
in order to harmonize the theories of Aristotle, Archimedes. Eratosthenes and Ptolemy as to the earth's circumference, so, these being exploded, similar illusions sprang up concerning leagues and, even in the
present day, are befogging the nautical history of the fifteenth and sixteenth centuries. None of the old authors or navigators suspect they
are dealing with a variable measure. The Pope and the treaty-makers,
as well as the seamen, give their distances, their sailing directions, in
leagues—just only leagues—without a qualifying adjective. In late
works, however, we read of leagues 14 $\frac{1}{6}$, 15, 16 $\frac{1}{2}$, 16 $\frac{2}{3}$, 17 $\frac{1}{2}$ and
21 $\frac{5}{8}$ to a degree, "Merveilleux procédé" writes D'Avezac, "qui, pour
" assurer l'exactitude du mesurage, crée la mesure même d'après l'objet
" bien ou mal mesuré."

It is in this respect that Mr. Harrisse's *Diplomatic History* will be
apt to mislead the unwary reader, and the danger is the greater because
of the mathematical top-dressing which gives a semblance of solidity to
what is really a quicksand of hypotheses. Thus we read—(p. 92) :

" Ferrer's above stated data result in four different lengths for his
" league, viz., 21·353, 21·813, 21·625 and 21·875 to the degree of the
" equator of his sphere. For reasons given in our notes we select from
" among these four valuations 21·875 to his equatorial degree upon which
" to base our calculations." Mr. Harrisse selected the right valuation
according to Eratosthenes, but, not according to Ferrer, for a reference

to Ferrer's statement (Appendix D) will show that he (Ferrer) did not give a valuation of 21·875 (21 $^7|_8$) but a valuation of 21·625 (21 $^5|_8$) leagues for his equinoctial degree. Ferrer's arithmetic was wrong according to his datum, and his other measurements are also wrong. The only one which concerns this inquiry is that on the latitude of the Cape Verde Islands, which he states to be 15°, and he gives the corresponding length of a degree on that parallel as 20 $^5|_8$ leagues ; whereas a correct calculation from the data of Eratosthenes (which he gives correctly enough) would make it 21 $^1_8$ (21·129) leagues. These are not four valuations of the *league,* but four valuations of the *degree.* It will be seen from the table (Appendix E) that Ferrer, in following Eratosthenes, made the globe one-sixth larger than it is, and in his statement (App. D, para. 10) it will also be seen that he knew very little about the ancient cosmographers : for he enumerates among his learned men "Ambrosi, Macrobi, Teodosi," as three distinct persons, whereas they are one, to wit, Aurelius Theodosius Macrobius, and, above all, he was wrong in assuming the 500 stades of Ptolemy and the 700 stades of Eratosthenes to express a degree of the same absolute length—to be in short identical concrete quantities. Of what value are the sines or tangents of such quantities as these ? Or what mathematical results can be based upon the statements of an authority who did not reason correctly, even from his own erroneous data ?

Again, with regard to Enciso, we read (at p. 105) that "in Enciso's "sphere, the value of the equatorial degree was 16·666 leagues," and lower down " Enciso's equatorial degree contained 18·0498 of his "leagues," and (at p. 192) the windrose in Enciso's *Suma,* "seems to "have been calculated on the basis of 17 $^1|_2$ leagues." Mr. Harrisse in this case thinks that "logic requires" him to select 16 $^2|_3$ leagues as the proper quantity. That is open to question, but here again, what value can such data as these have upon which to base a mathematical argument ?

It would be wrong, however, to suppose that Mr. Harrisse thinks he is dealing with real leagues. It is the inaccuracy of writing "leagues" of Enciso or Ferrer, etc., when he means "degrees" which is misleading. In a note at p. 193, he says, " The probability is that the league, which "is always a unit usual and fixed, was the same for Enciso and Ferrer ; " that is at the rate of 32 stades for one league." This throws an additional vagueness over the matter. It is like saying that it is *probable* that the three angles of a triangle are equal to two right angles, and then going on to argue impartially, by trigonometrical methods, on both hypotheses—that they are and that they are not thus equal. The effect is confusing and tends to reopen the theories of "fancy leagues" which were exploded by D'Avezac, forty years ago, in his discussion with Varnhagen.

The utter inapplicability of mathematical reasoning in questions such as these is further shown at p. 190, where Mr. Harrisse sets forth his mode of measuring the Cantino map and, after submitting it to mathematical methods, he concludes "that no reliance is to be placed " on the metrology of that map." Again, at p. 210, the Ribeiro map is put through a similar trigonometrical course and the conclusion is " that no reliance is to be placed, scientifically speaking, on the carto- " graphical statements of the period." The wonder is that the attempt was ever made ; but now that Mr. Harrisse has given it up we may, at least, hope that lesser authorities will cease their anachronistic efforts to scale off these crude and tentative maps of the old navigators as if they were admiralty charts or publications of the U. S. Geodetic Survey.

The *Suma de Geographia* of Fernandez de Enciso was published at Seville in 1519 and does, indeed, give the circumference of the earth as 6000 leagues. It was an estimation in round numbers, for it was equivalent to 24,000 Italian miles, and is found not only in Enciso but in some other authorities. That, divided by 360, gives $16\,^2|_3$ leagues to a degree or 16·666 as Mr. Harrisse states (p. 105). The reason, there- fore, of Mr. Harrisse's statement that "Enciso's equatorial degree con- " tained 18·0189 of his leagues" is not apparent and a careful perusal of the intricate calculations from pp. 193 to 197, in which Ferrer's leagues, and Enciso's leagues, and our marine leagues, are mingled with Greek stades and French metres fails to make it clear. The mixing up of absolute quantities such as leagues with shifting and unknown quanti- ties such as degrees is fatal to clear reasoning. No doubt the league both of Enciso and of Ferrer consists of 32 stades ; but Ferrer counted $21\,^7|_8$ and Enciso $16\,^2|_3$ of them to a degree. The quantities are irre- concilable and cannot be combined to form a third league. It is cer- tain that neither Enciso or any one else had a league of 18·0498 to a degree for there is not only his own statement as given above ; but his calculation of the distance between the port of Higueras and the island of San Thome, which he gives at 117 degrees and equivalent to 1950 leagues, and if one be divided into the other the quotient is again $16\,^2|_3$ leagues to a degree. The distances, at that time were inconceivably erroneous but the fact of this distance being over-estimated does not affect the ratio between the two quantities given.

Returning to the *Suma* of Enciso it must be observed that, when it was written, a more correct estimate of the length of a degree was very generally accepted and to this Enciso bears most decided testimony in that part of his book which may be called scientific, for it is in connection with a windrose and contains practical instructions for navigation, to the effect that in sailing on a direct northern course until the pole star is elevated one degree. "that degree is equal to seventeen leagues "and a half and that is the distance you will have gone." There is no uncertainty about that statement ; but Varnhagen and other advocates of "fancy leagues," in order to get leagues to suit their theories, started an idea that latitudinal and longitudinal degrees on a great circle of the earth were of different length. Enciso disposes of that idea. His sailing directions continue thus : "Also, if your course is one point the "distance sailed will be 17 $^3|_4$ leagues and departure 3 $^1|_2$ leagues for the "degree. If your course be two points, count the distance sailed 19 $^1|_6$

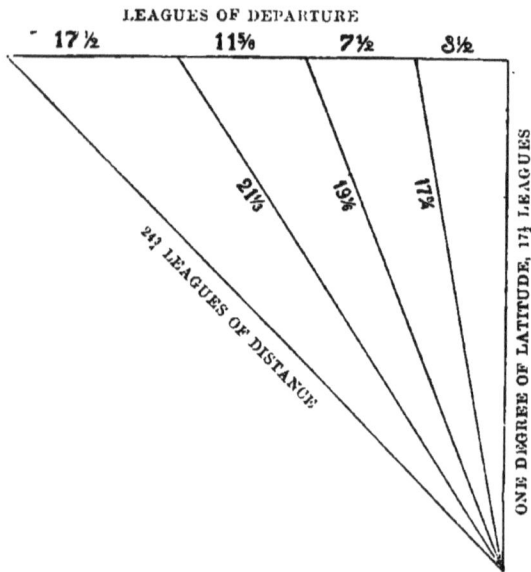

FIGURE 1.

"leagues and departure 7 $^1|_2$ leagues. If three points count the distance "sailed as 21 $^1|_3$ leagues and the departure 11 $^5|_6$ leagues. If the course "be four points count the distance as 24 $^3|_4$ leagues and the departure "17 $^1|_2$ leagues." The above diagram (Fig. 1) will show the meaning graphically .

Reference to a Traverse Table, in any work on navigation, will show these figures to be correct. For comparison, the statement in tabular form is as follows :—

One degree of Latitude 17½ leagues, by Enciso's windrose, is equal	LEAGUES.		
	Latitude One Degree.	Longitude or Departure.	Distance Sailed.
North by West ; Course 1 point W........	17½	3½	17¾
North-northwest ; Course 2 points W.....	17½	7½	19⅛
Northwest by North ; Course 3 points W..	17½	11⅝	21¼
Northwest ; Course 4 points W..........	17½	17½	24¾

Enciso's *Suma* is a rare book. There are four editions of it, A.D. 1519, 1530, 1530, 1546, all of which are in the Lenox Library and through the courtesy of the librarian, Mr. Wilberforce Eames, I am able to give the following tracing of the upper half of the windrose. (Fig. 2).

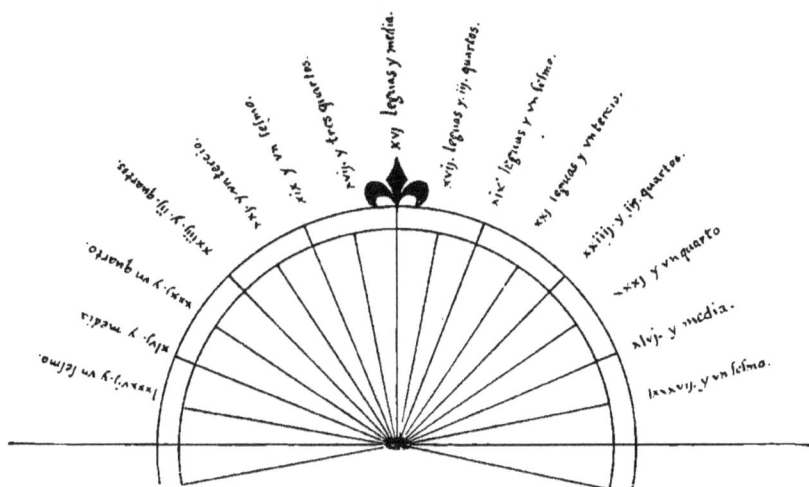

FIGURE 2.

Close inspection will show a misprint over the north point. A stroke is dropped and it reads XVI instead of XVII ; but it is clearly a misprint for the text underneath gives the distance at length *dezisiete leguas e media* seventeen leagues and a half. The error is corrected in the later editions. It is apparent by Fig. 1, for the course of four points is 45° and the triangle is right angled. For the preceding reasons it is evident that Enciso knew that the true length of a degree was 17 $\frac{1}{2}$ leagues, although the rate of 16 $\frac{2}{3}$ leagues was still held by many when he wrote. It will, I trust, be noted that all these sailors and cosmographers knew that the world was a sphere and in speculating upon the length of degrees of latitude and longitude they meant, as we do, degrees upon great circles unless they mention some specific latitude they are measuring upon.

I come now to inquire why the round number of 6000 leagues, or 24,000 Roman miles, should have been accepted as the measure of the circumference of the earth, and I find the answer in a letter of Amerigo Vespucci to Medici as follows : "The reason why I count 16 $\frac{2}{3}$ "leagues to a degree is that according to Ptolemy and Alfragan the "world is 24,000 miles in circumference which is equal to 6000 "leagues which divided by 360 is equal to 16 $\frac{2}{3}$ leagues, a result which "I have many times tested by the point of pilots and have found it "sound and true." The reason is, therefore, to be traced back to Ptolemy ; though by way of Alfragan, and it must be observed therefore, that it is a Greek, not an Arabian measurement.

It has been stated already that, when the Arabs overran the Eastern Roman Empire, they found in use a stade (Egyptian, royal, or Phileterian) of which 7 $\frac{1}{2}$ went to a Roman mile. They did not know that this measure did not arise until after Ptolemy's time and they divided the 500 stades of Ptolemy's degree by 7 $\frac{1}{2}$, and thus made it 66 $\frac{2}{3}$ Roman miles, which, in leagues of four to a mile, was equal to 16 $\frac{2}{3}$ leagues ; and this leads to a consideration of the effect the Arabian learning had on the cosmological ideas of the period now in review.

During the long ages of confusion in the West, while wave after wave of barbarians submerged the Roman civilization and the lamp of learning burned only in the seclusion of the cloister, the Arabians cultivated the arts and sciences at the chief centres of their power—Bagdad, Cairo and Cordova. The works of Aristotle, Archimedes, and Ptolemy, among other authors, were translated into Arabic for the great school of geography and astronomy founded at Bagdad, and about A.D. 833, the Caliph Almamoun ordered several measurements to be made of an arc of the meridian, the only attempt at a really scientific solution of the problem from the time of the Greeks until the beginning of the eighteenth century. Greek science first reached Western Europe through Arabic translations. The works of Massaudy and other Arabian geographers, passed into Spain through the Moors, and the *Celestial Movements* of Alfragan were translated into Latin and became well known to the learned. The measurements under Almamoun had resulted in an estimation of 56 $^2|_3$ miles to a degree and were accepted as true by Friar Bacon and Cardinal D'Ailly and others of the favourite authors of Columbus, who, dividing that figure by four, arrived at the conclusion he adhered to all his life that the length of a degree was 14 $^1|_6$ leagues, and he even asserted that he had verified it on one of his voyages to Guinea. It has not been absolutely proved that these Arabian miles were equivalent to Roman miles ; but the inquiry is long and it is sufficient now to say that they were taken to be equivalent, and in the belief that the earth was much smaller than it is, the admiral discovered America and thought it was India. In that way arose the belief, to which the admiral and his son adhered, in a degree of 14 $^1|_6$ leagues.

The different estimations of the length of a degree at the close of the fifteenth century can nearly all be traced back to some manipulation of Ptolemy's figures. If his 500 stades be divided by eight—the true divisor—we have another estimate often met with, viz., 62 $^1|_2$ miles to a degree or 15 $^5|_8$ leagues. This again, in current writing was rounded off to 60 miles and 15 leagues and given out also as Ptolemy's measurement. Jaime Ferrer alone followed Eratosthenes and valued the degree at 700 stades and, dividing by eight, he made it 87 $^1|_2$ miles ; this divided again by four made 21 $^7|_8$ leagues in reality, though by some error it is 21 $^5|_8$ in his opinion (App. D); but even he could not throw off the influence of Ptolemy and as pointed out already was driven to suppose that Ptolemy's 500 stades were longer and were equivalent to the 700 of Eratosthenes. There was in fact no settled estimate and we find in the opinion of Duran, Cabot and Vespucci, at Badajoz, that they quote Ptolemy for a length of 62 $^1|_2$ miles while themselves valuing a degree at 70 miles.

It is an anachronism to expect, in the writers of pre-scientific days, that precision of statement demanded by modern science and the reader must be prepared to meet with occasional passages which conflict with the general trend of the authorities. It is certain that Gomara held to the valuation of 17 $^1|_2$ leagues ; but he also quotes Ptolemy loosely, for he says (in Eden's translation) "He (Ptolemy) assigned likewise to " every degree three score miles which make seventeen Spanish leagues " and a half." Here are two manifest slips, because Ptolemy's degree was 62 $^1|_2$ miles and 17 $^1|_2$ leagues were 70 miles. This last valuation is beyond question ; for Fernan Columbus, in his official opinion at Badajoz, says expressly that "Castillian or marine leagues" are four miles in length. Again in a passage in the *Fifth Decade* of Peter Martyr we find that author complaining that sailors counted the 175 leagues, from Borneo to Malacca as ten degrees, whereas "the ancient

" philosophers reckoned 15 leagues or 60 miles to a degree." This passage shows how loosely Ptolemy was quoted, and also that the belief in 17 $\frac{1}{2}$ leagues to a degree had then been established at sea.

That which had been hidden from the learned throughout the ages, was revealed to the practical mariner unskilled in book lore ; but skilled to watch the elevation or sinking of the pole-star on a northern or southern course, and skilled also to estimate the dead reckoning of his little vessel by the aid of his sand glass. Therefore, when the length of voyages extended over thousands of miles, the elaborate measurements of the Greeks and Arabians were found to be wrong and the valuation of 17 $\frac{1}{2}$ leagues or 70 miles was accepted by sailors in advance of scholars. It was not far out of the way; since 70 Italian miles are equal to 64·3 English statute miles and 69·1 of these last miles are now reckoned to be the length of a degree of a great circle.

We may then conclude, with Navarrete and D'Avezac, that, at least as early as A.D. 1517, the valuation of 17 $\frac{1}{2}$ leagues had come into general use. Humboldt unhesitatingly quotes the leagues of Tordesillas at that rate. Herrera would seem to know of no other : for at the very outset of his *History*, he gives the circumference of the earth as 6,300 leagues. Magellan, writing in A.D. 1519, to King Ferdinand, stated that the island of San Antonio is 22° east of the line of demarcation. He gave the latitude at 17°, proving that he was reckoning at the rate of 17 $\frac{1}{2}$ leagues to an equatorial degree. At the convention of Badajoz, in A.D. 1524, Ruy de Villegas stated that he had measured a degree with that result, and Thomas Duran, Sebastian Cabot and Juan Vespucci, not only concurred in that valuation, but added that it was the usual estimate of Spanish and Portuguese sailors. While this was the opinion of the Spanish pilots and experts, the Spanish judges clung to the 62 $\frac{1}{2}$ miles of Ptolemy ; because they thought that the Portuguese were stretching out the distance to 70 miles for the purpose of including the Spice Islands within their line.

In A.D. 1529, at the treaty of Saragossa, the ratio of 17 $\frac{1}{2}$ leagues was admitted on both sides : for the Spaniards had recognized the fact that, as each party had 180 degrees, the length of a degree made no difference. It had to count on both sides, and in after years, whenever the treaty came up for discussion the same ratio was made the basis of argument. It persists all through the nautical authorities, not only in Spain, but in France : for we find that Champlain, in A.D. 1632, when giving instructions for making charts, laid down the rule that the scale must be 17 $\frac{1}{2}$ leagues to a degree.

The reader will see, from these remarks, that the old writers deal with only one league, that which was a multiple of the Roman mile.

The doubt was solely as to the number of these leagues in a degree. To write of leagues of Enciso, of Ferrer, or of anybody else, is to introduce uncertainty and error into the early history of this continent. It is most important to build up our history on a solid basis and to follow the tracks of the early voyagers along our shores with some degree of certainty. If then, the argument of this chapter be followed and accepted, the reader of the old narratives will have to do with only one league—the marine league used by Spanish, Portuguese, Italian and French sailors : not only at the time under review but for an indefinitely long period before and an indefinitely long time after. In the following table I give its equivalent value in English measures and, in order to show the limit of variation between the different authorities, I give also the value as taken by Captain Fox (on the authority of Rear Admiral Rogers of the U.S. Naval Observatory) for his calculations upon the landfall of Columbus. There is a difference of twelve feet in the mile. This will serve to show the close approximation of all the estimations made, and to explain the slight variations among them.

1 Roman or Italian mile = 1,618 yards = 4,854 feet English.
4   "   "   miles = 6,472   "   = 19,416 "   "
             or, according to Captain Fox,
1 Roman or Italian mile = 1,614 yards = 4,842 "   "
4   "   "   miles = 6,456   "   = 19,368 "   "
4 miles = 1 marine league of the early navigators.

The reader is again referred to Appendix E for a detailed table of the different views held concerning the subject of this chapter. These opinions are ranged in descending order, from Aristotle with a degree of 111·11 to Columbus with a degree of 45·33 of our modern nautical miles. The figures are given in Greek stades, Italian miles, and nautical miles. The equivalents in our nautical miles are printed for convenient reference in black faced type in the central columns.

IX.—THE LINES OF DEMARCATION ON THE OCEAN.

It has been shown that the line of demarcation, about which so much has been written during the past four hundred years—and so eloquently—is not the line of Pope Alexander. It is the line of the Spanish and Portuguese plenipotentiaries at Tordesillas, in A.D. 1494 the following year. They selected as their *terminus a quo* a group of islands—the Cape Verde Islands—extending over three degrees of longitude, without indicating which one they proposed to measure from and, in after years, in consequence, some measured from Bonavista, the eastern island, some from Fogo, the centre island, and some from San

Antonio, the western island ; according to the shifting political neces-
sities which from time to time arose. For reasons stated on a previous
page, the western island must be considered to be the legal point of
departure, and it—San Antonio—is in 17° 12′ of north latitude and
25° 5′ 7″ of west longitude.

Upon reflection, it will appear that there are only two inquiries
concerning the location of the line of demarcation which can yield any
result of historical interest. First, where does this line fall under
present conditions of nautical science ? and second, where was it supposed to fall by the Spaniards and Portuguese governments, under the
conditions existing at the time of the treaty, or as near as possible to
it ? This latter problem may be solved by the aid of maps ; but
not by weaving a tissue of hypotheses out of Jaime Ferrer's errors or
by performing mathematical processes on globes of imaginary dimen-
sions. If the distances had been stated in degrees the case would be
different, but the Pope and the plenipotentiaries avoided degrees and
laid down the distance in leagues. The degree is a relative term of
length having no intrinsic value but depending on the circle of which
it is the three hundred and sixtieth part. It is the same on a library
globe as on the globe of the earth—the league is a definite concrete
quantity independent of globes or circles. The terrestrial globe of
Ferrer was 252,000 stades in circumference ; Enciso had two sizes in
his *Suma*, one (which Mr. Harrisse adopts) of 192,000 stades, and another which he gave out to practical sailors of 201,600 stades ; Columbus imagined a globe of 163,200 stades only, and to that he clung all
his life. It is manifest that 370 leagues measured upon four globes so
different in magnitude would extend over greatly different numbers of
degrees, and when all these varying quantities are combined with
others as problematical and turned round in a mathematical kaleido-
scope, the effect is bewildering.

Returning to the first question, I would repeat that the real latitude
of the island of San Antonio is 17° 12′ north, and would add that, on
that parallel, degrees of longitude are 57·32 of our nautical miles in
length. It has been shown, on previous pages, that four Roman or old
Italian miles, of 1618 English yards each, were reckoned to a league,
and therefore, the 370 leagues of Tordesillas multiplied by four were
1480 Italian miles. As the English nautical mile contains 2029 English yards, the following sum in simple arithmetic will tell us what
these leagues are in our familiar measure :—

yds.		yds.			Ital. miles.		Eng. naut. miles.
2029	:	1618	:	:	1480	:	1180·2

The 370 leagues are, therefore, equivalent to 1180 of our marine
miles, omitting the fraction.

It has been stated that on the parallel of San Antonio a degree of longitude is 57·32 nautical miles. We have, therefore, to divide one quantity by the other, thus—

$$1180·2 \div 57·32 = 20°\ 35',$$

and the equivalent in longitude is therefore 20° 35'. To find this point on our charts the longitude west from Greenwich of the starting point must be added and the longitude of San Antonio is 25° 5', and

$$25°\ 5' + 20°\ 35' = 45°\ 40'\ \text{west longitude};$$

so that if we draw a line on an admiralty chart at the meridian of 45° 40', it will be the true line of the treaty of Tordesillas, and we shall find that the line of demarcation, if calculated on true data, would never have touched any point on the continent of North America. Cape Race is its most eastern point and is in longitude 53° 4' W. So the true line of Tordesillas passes 7° 24' seaward of it and cuts the coast of Greenland in Davis' Strait. The Dominion of Canada is thus shut up in the Spanish demarcation and only the neglected John Cabot, over whose unknown tomb memory has raised no trophies, has saved us from the full force of the primary count in the Venezuelan argument.

Coming now to the second point of our inquiry, it must be admitted that, to all intents and purposes, this line of Tordesillas did at the period under review, cut our coasts ; since both the Spaniards and Portuguese thought it did and governed themselves accordingly. As explained before, the present paper is not concerned with South America ; but the map in front of Mr. Harrisse's *History* contains the results of his calculations on the "spheres" of Ribeiro, Ferrer, Enciso, Oviedo, Cantino and the Badajoz experts, transferred to our admiralty charts, and they show lines of west longitude from 42° 30' to 49° 25', so that in any of these worlds the line would have passed seawards, by nearly four degrees, of Cape Race ; but, what is more remarkable, the unexpected result appears that Jaime Ferrer with a world of 252,000 stades, and Enciso with a world of 201,600 stades, should have come out to within one mile of each other as mathematically calculated by Mr. Harrisse. It is also worthy of remark that the present writer, working upon the world as now known of 216,000 stades in circumference, by simple arithmetic and with modern data, should have arrived within three miles of the same conclusion. Stated in Italian miles the lines are as follows : in the present paper with a degree of 75 miles at 45° 40' ; Enciso in Mr. Harrisse's map with a degree of 66·66 miles at 45° 38', and Ferrer on the same map with a degree of 87·5 miles at 45° 37'. This is a very surprising result of mathematical reasoning. It means in effect that whether 370 leagues (equal to 1180 Italian miles) are divided by 75, 87·5 or 66·6, the quotient is the same within a limit of only 3 minutes of longitude.

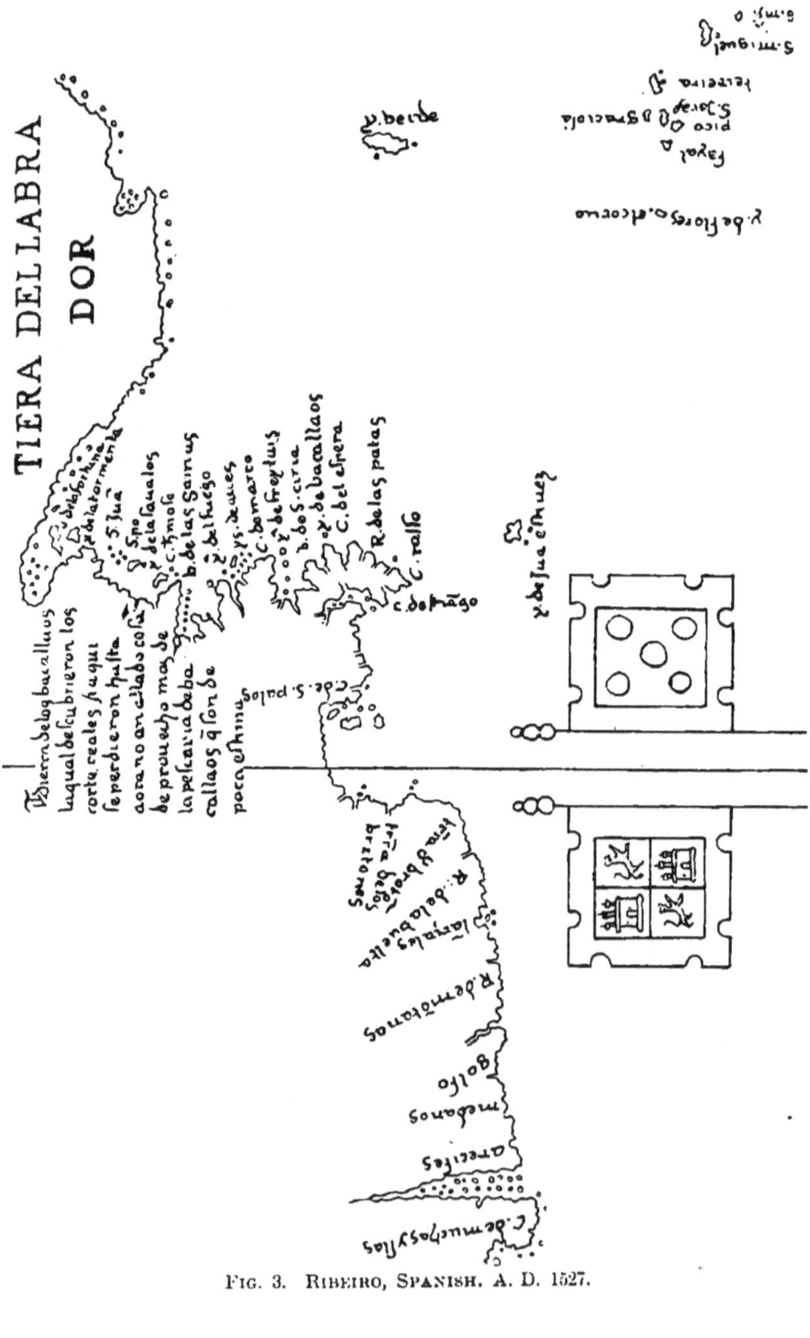

FIG. 3. RIBEIRO, SPANISH. A. D. 1527.

The second point of our inquiry, namely, where upon our coast did those old navigators think that the line touched ? cannot be found mathematically, for it would seem from these calculations on "spheres" that the same result is reached from widely different data. That method is plainly inapplicable. It is necessary, therefore, to turn to the maps of the period—those maps which, mathematically measured, will mislead the student ; but which will yield valuable information to whoever will read them in the light of their own age. The topographical features upon them will show within a very small distance the place where the line of Tordesillas touched our coast— in the current opinion of the period when the people were alive who had the practical settlement of it.

The Spanish view is set forth in two maps, both copied from the official map of Spain. One is by Diego Ribeiro and is dated A.D. 1529, the other is dated A.D. 1527, and has been ascribed to Fernan Columbus, but Mr. Harrisse thinks it to be the work of Nuno Garcia de Toreno. Mr. Harrisse has the greater probability on his side ; but it makes little difference, since both Ribeiro and Garcia were celebrated pilots and were among the experts on behalf of Spain at the Badajoz conference. Both of them were distinguished chart makers and Ribeiro was one of the commissioners for compiling and supervising the standard map— (Padron Real). Fig. 3 is an extract from the well known map at Weimar made by him. The two flags are on the South American coast

FIG. 4. NUNO GARCIA, SPANISH, A. D. 1527.

and have been moved up and included in this extract to show how the line is marked on the map—the Portuguese to the east and the Spanish to the west of the dividing line between them. The reader's attention is called to the fact that the line cuts the coast far west of Cape Race and westward of the islands on the south coast of Newfoundland. It passes west of nearly the whole region of Baccallaos and just clears what may be taken as Nova Scotia and the point of Cape Breton. It corresponds as nearly as possible to the meridian of 60° W. on our charts which passes through Cabot Strait close to the island of St. Paul.

Fig. 4 is an outline extract of the map by Nuno Garcia, or Fernan Columbus. It is traced from Winsor's *Narr. and Crit. History*, Vol. II, p. 43. In this map the opening between Cape Breton and Newfoundland is indicated, as it is also on earlier maps, and the line of demarcation passes through it. These two maps are conclusive evidence that, on the Spanish official map, the division was close to the point of Cape Breton and cut off all Newfoundland into the Portuguese demarcation. That then was the Spanish view of the question, and it is important to remember that the true longitude of the line has been shown to be 45° 40′. The longitude, therefore, on both these maps is 14° 20′ out of the truth; so far as that part of the coast is concerned.

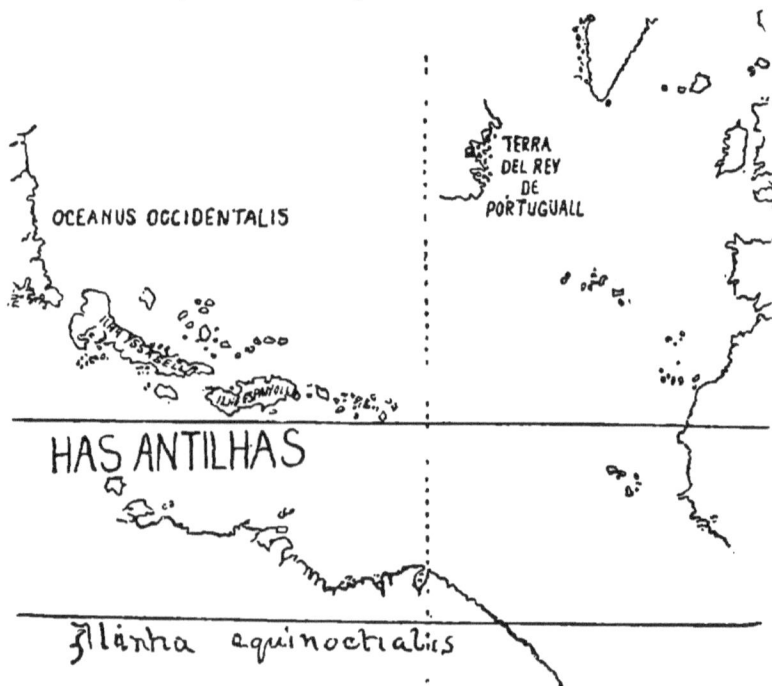

FIG. 5. CANTINO MAP, PORTUGUESE, A. D. 1502.

Turning now to the other side, there will be found only two maps of undoubted Portuguese origin in which the line is shown. The first in order of date is the Cantino map of A.D. 1502, which has been beautifully reproduced in Mr. Harrisse's work on the *Corte Reales.* Fig. 5 is an outline tracing of a portion of this map. The coast of America at that early date is not continuous and much distorted ; but it is plainly manifest that the dotted line on the sketch, representing the dividing line, passes far west of Cape Race and cuts off all of Newfoundland to the east. This map, therefore, concurs with the Spanish maps above cited. The longitude of this map is, therefore, just as erroneous (and no more so) as that of the Spanish maps, and it will also be observed that every one of the Antilles is north of the tropic of Cancer : whereas, in reality, every one of them lies to the south of it. The latitude, therefore, of that part of the map is from eight to ten degrees out of the truth.

Fig. 6 is the second Portuguese map referred to above. It is anonymous and undated ; but all authorities agree in assigning it to A.D. 1514-1520. The extract given is taken from Kohl and in it we have the most indubitable corroboration of the indications upon the three maps previously cited. The line is seen to cut off Baccalaos to the east. It just grazes the point of Nova Scotia and passes to the north at the precise point where Cabot Strait opens up in the rear of Newfoundland.

Here, then, we have a most striking record of concurrence, between the Spanish and Portuguese authorities, as to where, in their opinion, the line of Tordesillas cut our coast. We are not called upon to perform elaborate mathematical calculations upon imaginary worlds of different sizes and everyone of them wrong, nor to measure distances in leagues of various lengths or in degrees of different great circles, containing from 56 to 87 miles each. The opinion current at the time. which was the subject of our second question, is set forth graphically beyond possibility of doubt. As I have urged in previous papers. Cape Race is the cardinal point of the geography of the northeast coast of America. and always has been. The very same name has clung to it since A.D. 1502, and, in all the four cartographical witnesses above cited, the line passes at an approximately similar distance west of it. If then the question be asked, where the line of Tordesillas really was ? I would reply, at 45° 40' W. on our maps ; but if the question be—where did the Spaniards and Portuguese suppose it to be ? I should answer—close to the west of the meridian of 60° on our maps.

I have called attention to the fact that these old maps are very erroneous as to longitude ; and sometimes as to latitude also. How

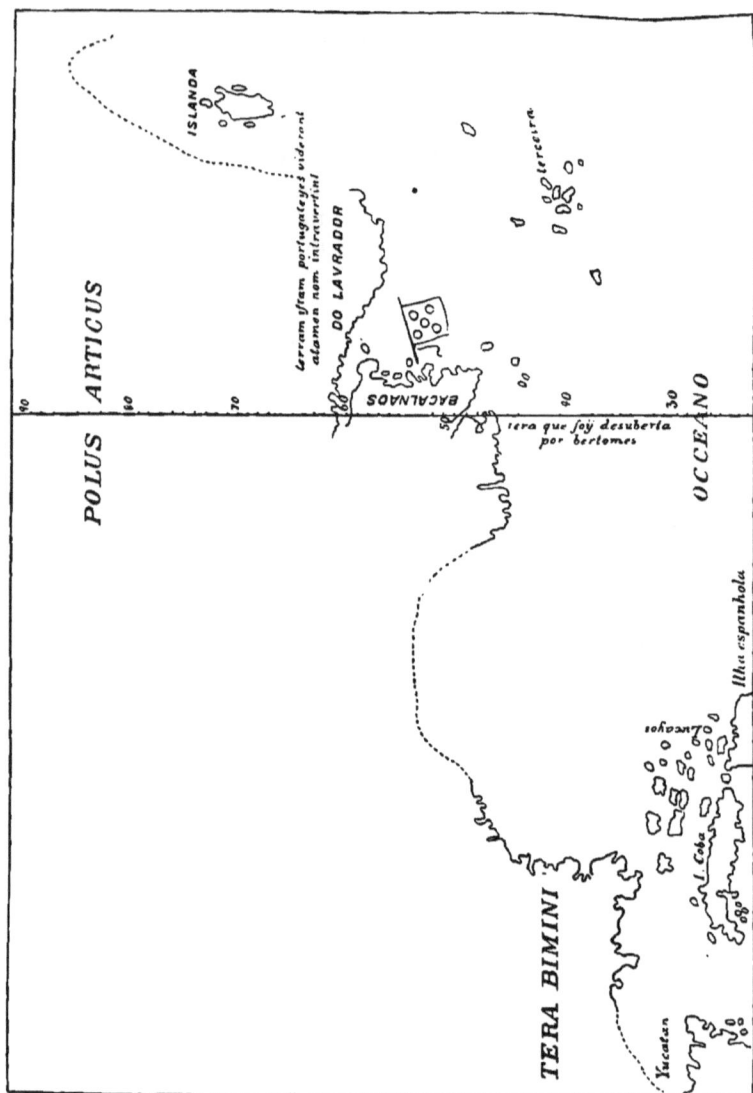

FIG. 6. PORTUGUESE MAP, A. D. 1514-20.

could they possibly be correct when the old navigators had no means
of correcting their dead reckoning ? Hence it was that, in measuring their course south and east to the Moluccas round the Cape of Good
Hope and over the Indian Ocean, their estimations of longitude differed
by as much as forty-six degrees. If, as has been stated above, the
Mediterranean Sea, which washed their feet from childhood, was always
laid down twenty degrees too long, ought it to be cause for wonder if,
across the unquiet western ocean, their longitude was fifteen degrees
in error ?

Elsewhere, I have endeavoured to point out the injustice to the
memory of Sebastian Cabot in calling him false and venal for changing
his service, as did so many of the great sailors of those days without
blame. The concurrence of the line of partition on these maps clears
the memory of that most daring of sailors, Corte Reale, from the charge
of "wantonly" inscribing Newfoundland on his maps "as within the
"dominions of Portugal." He did not make the Cantino map, and,
if that map was based on his information, the information is confirmed
by the Spanish maps twenty-five years later. Nor can it be said that
the Spanish cartographers were misled by him ; for their maps were
based on the reports of Estevan Gomez, who spent ten months along
the east coast of America in A.D. 1525.

There are also very weighty historical reasons which confirm the
above conclusion as to the point of contact between the two spheres of
influence. When John Cabot was preparing to sail to the west, King
Ferdinand, in a letter to De Puebla (March 28, 1496), objected to the
expedition as being in prejudice to "our rights or those of the King of
"Portugal." Afterwards, in A.D. 1511, the King's orders to Juan de
Agramonte, relative to Cabot, manifest a doubt as to which side of the
line the discovery was on. He was ordered to take Breton pilots ;
thus clearly indicating the locality to be in the "Bay of the Bretons,"
in the region marked on the Portuguese chart Fig. 6, as " the land discovered by the Bretons;" and he is to make a settlement there, without infringing on the rights of Portugal. This last condition confirms
the maps that the point of contact was in the King's opinion near the
spot of Cabot's discovery as laid down subsequently in Sebastian Cabot's
map of 1544.

Again, in A.D. 1541, when Spanish spies reported the preparations
for Roberval's proposed settlement, the Spanish ambassador at Lisbon
endeavoured to incite the King of Portugal to send an expedition to
destroy these French interlopers. The King replied that he knew
where the French were going and that it was in his territory ; but he
declined to take action because they could do him no harm there, and

he thought, moreover, the expedition would fail. The ambassador then addressed himself to the queen, who was devoted to the interests of the Emperor Charles V., and even suggested that, if the King would not defend his territories, they should be ceded to the Emperor who would take care of them. This expedition was to sail through Cabot Strait and make a settlement within it.

The grant of the King of Portugal in 1521 to Joam Alvarez Fagundez was for the territory "from the line of demarcation on the "south to the boundaries of the land discovered by Corte Reale on the "north," and, if the map of Lazaro Luis of A.D. 1563 is to be accepted as evidence of a grant forty years before, it would seem that a part of the peninsula of Nova Scotia was considered to be within the Portuguese line.

We may, therefore, feel sure, both on cartographical and historical grounds, that although the line of demarcation, according to the light of the astronomical science of the present day, would pass away out to sea seven degrees westward of this continent, yet as between Spain and Portugal, it was acknowledged to cut the coast of Nova Scotia and that Portugal by right of prior occupation might have held the territory of Baccallaos as against Spain. By right of discovery England's claim was prior to all : for John Cabot touched the main continent in 1497. The point where he touched is indicated by the instructions of Ferdinand to Juan de Agramonte above cited. It was close to the line of demarcation and, on the map of Sebastian Cabot of 1544, it was at Cape Breton. This last point has been sufficiently elucidated by the present writer in previous papers in these *Transactions*. It only remains to observe that converging lines of inquiry concentrate the interest of geographical historians upon that point of the northeast coast of Nova Scotia. Those who seek for mathematical demonstration in history will lose their labour. The subject matter admits of probable proof alone. Even if the probability should amount to moral certainty, its intrinsic nature will be the same. An erroneous quantity propounded to a calculating machine can produce nothing but an erroneous result and hypotheses worked out by mathematical tables acquire no higher probability on that account. The tendency is in the reverse direction.

NOTES.

1 Maine—Ancient Law, p. 101.

2 Cicero—de Legibus, Bk. ii, chap. 4.

3 Bryce—Holy Roman Empire, p. 244.

4 Maine—Ancient Law, p. 249.

5 St. Augustine—de Civitate Dei, xvi., 5.

6 Harrisse—Diplomatic History, p. 76.

7 Lingard—History of England, vol. 2, p. 178.

8 Harrisse—Diplomatic History, p. 17.

9 André—Manuel de Droit Canon, *ad verb.*

10 Harrisse—Diplomatic History, p. 18.

11 Harrisse—Diplomatic History, p. 19.

12 Harrisse—Diplomatic History, *ib.*

13 Harrisse—Diplomatic History, *ib.*

14 This *Campo di Fiori* is the place indicated at p. 51 *Diplomatic History* as " the Floral Field." It is an open space off the Piazza Navona where acts of public proclamation were made.

15 Humboldt—Examên Critique, III., p. 52 *note.*

16 Humboldt—Cosmos, II., p. 657.

17 It is impossible to make references to all the authorities from whence the conclusions of this chapter have been drawn. Many are cited in the text. Among those not so mentioned are Humboldt, *Cosmos* and *Examen Critique ;* Bunbury, Ancient Geography; Beasley, Dawn of Modern Geography; Smith, Dictionary of Greek and Roman Antiquities and other works of the same class ; Bulletin de la Société de Géographie ; articles by D'Avezac and Varnhagen.

APPENDIX A.

THE BULL OF DEMARCATION (C) OF MAY 4, 1493 (INTER CETERA), COLLATED WITH THE SUPPRESSED DRAFT (A) OF MAY 3.

The following is a copy of the Bull as found in the *Fonti Italiani*, Part III. of the series of volumes issued by the *Reale Commissione Colombiana*, Rome, 1894. Those words which were not in the unpromulgated Bull and were inserted to bring it to its final form, as published, are printed in italics. The words in the draft which were omitted in the final Bull are printed in the footnotes with references to their original places in the text.

ALEXANDER episcopus, servus servorum Dei, carissimo in Christo filio Ferdinando regi et carissimæ in Christo filiæ Helisabeth reginæ Castellæ, Legionis, Aragonum, *Siciliae* et Granatæ illustribus, salutem et apostolicam benedictionem. Inter cetera divinæ majestati beneplacita opera et cordis nostri desiderabilia illud profecto potissimum existit, ut fides catholica et christiana religio nostris præsertim temporibus exaltetur ac ubilibet amplietur et dilatetur, animarumque salus procuretur, ac barbaræ nationes deprimantur et ad fidem *ipsam*[1] reducantur. Unde cum ad hanc sacram Petri Sedem, divina favente clementia, meritis licet imparibus, evocati fuerimus, cognoscentes vos tanquam veros catholicos reges et principes, quales semper fuisse novimus, et a vobis præclare gesta toti pene jam orbi notissima demonstrant, ne dum id exoptare, sed omni conatu, studio et diligentia, nullis laboribus, nullis impensis nullisque parcendo periculis, etiam proprium sanguinem effundendo, efficere, ac omnem animum vestrum omnesque conatus ad hoc jam dudum dedicasse, quemadmodum recuperatio regni Granatæ a tyrannide Saracenorum hodiernis temporibus per vos cum tanta divini nominis gloria facta, testatur ; digne ducimur non immerito et debemus illa vobis *etiam* sponte et favorabiliter concedere, per quæ hujusmodi sanctum et laudabile ac immortali Deo Acceptum propositum in dies ferventiori animo, ad ipsius Dei honorem et imperii christiani propagationem prosequi valeatis. Sane accepimus quod vos, qui dudum animo proposueratis aliquas insulas et terras *firmas* remotas et incognitas ac per alios hactenus non repertas quærere et invenire, ut illarum incolas et habitatores ad colendum Redemptorem nostrum et fidem catholicam profitendam reduceretis, hactenus in expugnatione et recuperatione ipsius regni Granatæ plurimum occupati, hujusmodi sanctum et laudabile propositum vestrum ad optatum finem perducere nequivistis. Sed tandem, sicut Domino placuit, regno prædicto recuperato, volentes desiderium adimplere vestrum, dilectum filium Christoforum Colon, *virum utique dignum et plurimum commendandum ac tanto negotio aptum,* cum navigiis et hominibus ad similia instructis, non sine maximis laboribus et periculis ac expensis destinastis, ut terras *firmas et insulas* remotas et incognitas hujusmodi per mare, ubi hactenus navigatum non fuerat, diligenter inquireretis. Qui tandem, divino auxilio, facta extrema diligentia,[2] in mari Oceano navigantes, certas insulas remotissimas et etiam terras firmas, quæ per alios hactenus repertæ non fuerant, invenerunt; in quibus quamplurimæ gentes pacifice viventes et, ut asseritur, nudi incedentes, nec carnibus vescentes, inhabitant ; et, ut præfati nuntii vestri possunt opinari, gentes ipsæ in insulis et terris prædictis habitantes credunt unum Deum creatorem in cœlis esse, ac ad fidem catholicam amplexandum et bonis moribus im-

---

buendum satis apti videntur; spesque habetur quod, si erudirentur, nomen
salvatoris domini nostri Yhesu Christi in terris et insulis prædictis facile
induceretur.   Ac præfatus Christoforus in una ex principalibus insulis
prædictis jam unam turrim satis munitam, in qua certos Christianos, qui
secum iverant, in custodiam, et ut alias insulas et terras *firmas* remotas et
incognitas inquirerent, posuit, construi et edificari fecit; in quibus quidem
insulis et terris jam repertis aurum, aromatha et aliæ quam plurimæ res
pretiosæ diversi generis et diversæ qualitatis reperiuntur : unde omnibus
diligenter et præsertim fidei catholicæ exaltatione et dilatatione, prout decet
catholicos reges et principes, consideratis, more progenitorum vestrorum
claræ memoriæ regum, terras *firmas* et insulas prædictas illarumque incolas
et habitatores vobis, divina favente clementia, subjicere et ad fidem catholicam reducere proposuistis. Nos igitur hujusmodi vestrum *sanctum* et laudabile propositum plurimum in Domino commendantes, ac cupientes ut illud
ad debitum finem perducatur, et ipsum nomen Salvatoris nostri in partibus
illis inducatur, hortamur vos plurimum in Domino, et per sacri lavacri sus-
ceptionem, qua mandatis apostolicis obligati estis, et viscera misericordiæ
domini nostri Yhesu Christi attente requirimus, ut cum expeditionem hujusmodi omnino prosequi et assumere prona mente orthodoxæ fidei zelo inten-
datis, populos in hujusmodi insulis *et terris* degentes ad christianam
religionem[1] suscipiendam inducere velitis et debeatis, nec pericula, nec labores
ullo unquam tempore vos deterreant, firma spe fidutiaque conceptis quod
Deus omnipotens conatus vestros feliciter prosequetur. Et ut tanti negotii
provintiam, apostolicæ gratiæ largitate *donati*,[2] liberius et audatius assuma-
tis, motu proprio, non ad vestram vel alterius pro vobis super hoc nobis
oblatæ petitionis instantiam, sed de nostra mera liberalitate et ex certa
scientia ac de apostolicæ potestatis plenitudine, *omnes*[3] *insulas et terras firmas
inventas et inveniendas, detectas et detegendas, versus occidentem et meridiem,
fabricando et constituendo unam lineam a polo artico, scilicet septemtrione, ad
polum antarticum, scilicet meridiem, sive terrae firmae et insulae inventae et
inveniendae sint versus Indiam aut versus aliam quamcumque partem: quae linea
distet a qualibet insularum quae vulgariter nuncupantur de los Azores et Caboverde centum leucis versus occidentem et meridiem, ita quod omnes insulae et
terrae firmae repertae et reperiendae, detectae et detegendae, a praefata linea versus
occidentem et meridiem per alium regem aut principem christianum non fuerint
actualiter possessae usque ad diem nativitatis domini nostri Yhesu Christi
proxime praeteritum, a quo incipit annus praesens MCCCCLXXXX. tertius, quando
fuerint per nuntios et capitaneos vestros inventae aliquae praedictarum insularum,*
auctoritate omnipotentis Dei nobis in beato Petro concessa ac vicariatus
Yhesu Christi qua fungimur in terris, cum omnibus illarum dominiis[4] civitatibus, castris, locis et villis, juribusque et jurisdictionibus ac pertinentiis
universis, vobis hæredibusque et successoribus vestris, Castellæ et Legionis
regibus, in perpetuum[5] tenore præsentium, donamus, concedimus, et assigna-
mus, vosque et hæredes ac successores præfatos[6] illarum dominos cum plena[7]
libera et omnimoda potestate, auctoritate et jurisdictione facimus, constituimus et deputamus ; decernentes nihilominus per hujusmodi donationem,
concessionem *et* assignationem[8] nostram nulli christiano principi, *qui actualiter praefatas insulas aut terras firmas possederit usque ad praedictum diem nativitatis domini nostri Yhesu Christi,* jus quæsitum, sublatum intelligi posse aut
auferri debere. Et insuper mandamus vobis, in virtute sanctæ obedientiæ
ut, sicut etiam pollicemini, et non dubitamus pro vestra maxima devotione
et regia magnanimitate vos esse facturos, ad terras *firmas* et insulas prædictas
viros probos et Deum timentes, doctos, peritos et expertos ad instruendum
incolas et habitatores præfatos in fide catholica et in bonis moribus imbuen-

---

[1] Substitute, professionem (for religionem .
[2] Substitute, donatis (for donati).
[3] Substitute, et singulas terras et insulas prædictas sic incognitas et hactenus per nuncios vestros
repertas et reperiendas in posterum quæ sub dominio actuali temporali aliquorum dominorum
Christianorum constitutæ non sint.
[4] Insert, cum.
[5] Insert, auctoritate apostolica.
[6] Insert, de illis investimus, illarumque.
[7] Insert, et.
[8] Insert, et investituram.

dum, destinare debeatis, omnem debitam diligentiam in præmissis adhibentes ; ac quibuscumque personis' cujuscumque dignitatis, *etiam imperialis et regalis*, status, gradus, ordinis vel conditionis, sub excommunicationis latæ sententiæ pœna, quam eo ipso, si contrafecerint, incurrant, districtius inhibemus, ne ad insulas et terras² *firmas inventas et inveniendas, detectas et detegendas, versus occidentem et meridiem, fabricando et constituendo lineam a polo artico ad polum antarticum, sive terrae firmae et insulae inventao et inveniendae sint versus Indiam aut versus aliam quamcumque partem, quae linea distet a qualibet insularum quae vulgariter nuncupantur de los Azores et Caboverde centum leucis versus occidentem et meridiem, ut praefertur*, pro mercibus habendis vel quavis alia de causa accedere præsumant absque vestra ac hæredum et successorum vestrorum prædictorum licentia speciali ; ³ non obstantibus constitutionibus et ordinationibus apostolicis' ceterisque contrariis quibuscumque; in illo a quo imperia et dominationes ac bona cuncta procedunt, confidentes, quod dirigente Domino actus vestros, si hujusmodi sanctum et laudabile *propositum⁵* prosequamini, brevi tempore, cum felicitate et gloria totius populi christiani, vestri labores et conatus exitum felicissimum consequentur. Verum, quia difficile foret præsentes litteras ad singula quæque loca in quibus expediens fuerit deferri, volumus, ac motu et scientia similibus decernimus, quod illarum transumptis, manu publici notarii inde rogati subscriptis et sigillo alicujus personæ in ecclesiastica dignitate constitutæ, seu curiæ ecclesiasticæ, munitis, ea prorsus fides in judito et extra ac alias ubilibet adhibeatur, quæ præsentibus adhiberetur, si essent exhibitæ vel ostensæ. Nulli ergo omnino hominum liceat hanc paginam nostræ *commendationis*, hortationis, requisitionis, donationis, concessionis, assignationis,⁶ constitutionis, deputationis, *decreti*, mandati, inhibitionis⁷ *et* voluntatis,⁸ infringere, vel ei ausu temerario contraire. Si quis autem hoc attentare præsumpserit, indignationem omnipotentis Dei ac beatorum Petri et Pauli apostolorum ejus se noverit incursurum.

Datum Romæ, apud sanctum Petrum, anno incarnationis dominicæ MCCCCLXXXXIII. quarto nonas maii, pontificatus nostri anno primo.

---

¹ Insert, etiam.
² Insert, prædita postquam per vestros nuntios seu ad id missos inventæ et receptæ fuerint.
³ Insert—Et quia etiam nonnulli Portugalliæ reges in partibus Africe, Guineæ et Mineræ auri alias insulas, similiter, etiam ex concessione apostolica eis facta repererunt et acquisiverunt et per sedem apostolicam eis diversa privilegia, gratiæ, libertates, immunitates, exentiones et indulta concessa fuerunt. Nos, vobis ac hæredibus et subcesoribus vestris prædictis, ut insulis et terris per vos repertis, et reperiendis hujusmodi, omnibus et singulis gratiis, privilegiis, exentionibus libertatibus facultatibus immunitatibus et indultis hujusmodi, quorum omnium tenores ac si de verbo ad verbum præsentibus insererentur, haberi volumus pro sufficienter expressis et insertis, uti, potiri et gaudere libere et licite possitis ac debeatis in omnibus et per omnia, perinde ac si vobis ac hæredibus et subcesoribus prædictis specialiter concessa fuissent. motu, auctoritate, scientia, et apostolicæ potestatis plenitudine similibus, de specialis dono gratiæ, indulgemus, illaque in omnibus et per omnia ad vos hæredes ac subcesores vestros prædictos extendimus pariter et ampliamus.
⁴ Insert—Nec non omnibus illis, quæ in litteris desuper editis concessa sunt non obstare.
⁵ Substitute, negotium (for propositum).
⁶ Insert, investituræ, facti.
⁷ Insert, indulti extensionis, ampliationis.
⁸ Insert, et decreti.

TRANSLATION.

Alexander, Bishop, Servant of the Servants of God, to his very dear son in Christ, Ferdinand, King; and to his very dear daughter in Christ, Isabella, Queen, illustrious, of Castile, Leon, Aragon, Sicily, Granada, health and apostolic benediction. Among the works most acceptable to the Divine Majesty, and desirable to our hearts, that is certainly above all, that the Catholic faith, and the Christian religion, especially in our times, should be exalted and everywhere diffused and spread; and that the salvation of souls be sought after, and barbarous nations subjected, and brought over to the said faith. Wherefore We, having been elevated, by the favour of divine clemency, although undeserving by our merits of so high a rank, to this sacred seat of Peter, acknowledging you, as true catholic Kings and Princes, whom we have always known as such and as your most illustrious actions now made known to all the world shew, not only that you are desirous of that, but that you likewise prosecute it with all vigour, earnestness, and diligence, sparing no fatigue, expense, or danger whatever, even to the shedding of your blood, and that it is long since you have dedicated all your mind and all your efforts to it, as the recovery of the kingdom of Granada from the tyranny of the Saracens, recently effected by you, with such evident proofs of divine favour, clearly shews; we deem it, therefore, worthy of us, and are bound to grant you even spontaneously and graciously, those things, by which you may be enabled more fervently to follow up this holy and praiseworthy resolution, and acceptable to the eternal God, to the honour of God, and for the propagation of the Christian empire. And in truth it has come to our knowledge, that you, who had resolved in your minds, for some time past, to seek for and discover some remote and unknown islands and main-lands, and by no others hitherto found out, in order to induce the natives and inhabitants of them to worship our Redeemer and to profess the Catholic faith, but had not until now been able to conduct this holy and praiseworthy resolution to its wished-for end, finding yourselves fully engaged in the conquest and recovery of the said kingdom of Granada ; but at length, as it pleased the Lord, having recovered the foresaid kingdom, and wishing to fulfil your desires, you despatched our beloved son Christopher Columbus, a man every way worthy and deserving of great praise, and capable of so great an affair, with vessels and men accustomed to such undertakings, with very great labour, danger and expense, in order that he might diligently seek out those main-lands and remote and unknown islands, in a sea where no person had navigated until now. Who, at last, with the assistance of God, having used extreme diligence, in navigating through the ocean, discovered certain very remote islands, and also main-lands, that nobody had as yet found out; the inhabitants of which are numerous, live peacefully, and, as it is affirmed, go naked, and feed not upon flesh; and as far as your foresaid messengers can opine, the people who inhabit the foresaid islands and lands, believe that there is in heaven a God Creator ; and appear well disposed to embrace the Catholic faith, and civilized manners; and there is a hope, that if they were instructed, the name of our Lord and Saviour Jesus Christ would be introduced into the said lands and islands. And already the said Christopher has caused to be constructed and built in one of the principal of the foresaid islands, a very strong tower, in which he placed certain Christians, who went out with him, in order that they might have the care of it, and likewise discover other remote and unknown islands and continents. In which islands and lands already discovered, are to be found, gold, spices, and a great many other precious things of divers kinds and qualities. Whence, having diligently considered all these things, and especially the advancement and spreading of the Catholic faith, as it becomes Catholic Kings and Princes, you have resolved, in imitation of the Kings your ancestors of renowned memory, with the favour of the divine clemency, to subject and reduce to the Catholic faith the foresaid main-lands and islands, and the natives and

inhabitants of the same. We therefore, highly commending in the name
of God your holy and laudable resolution, and wishing that it may be con-
ducted to the desired end, and the name of our Saviour introduced into
those parts, exhort you warmly in the Lord, and by the holy baptism you
have received, by which you subjected yourselves to the apostolic commands, and by the bowels of the mercy of our Lord Jesus Christ, earnestly
intreat you to proceed in taking up and prosecuting completely this expedition, the zeal for the orthodox faith continuing in you, you will and ought to
induce the people, who inhabit the foresaid islands and continents, to embrace the Christian religion; nor let the dangers and fatigues of it ever deter
you, possessing the firmest hope and confidence, that God omnipotent will
happily accompany all your undertakings.   And in order that you may
undertake more freely and boldly the charge of so great an affair, given to
you with the liberality of apostolic grace, We of our own motion, and
not at your solicitation, nor upon petition presented to Us upon this subject by other persons in your name, but of our pure free will and certain
knowledge, and with the plentitude of apostolic power, by the authority of
God omnipotent granted to Us through blessed Peter, and of the vicarship
of Jesus Christ, which we exercise upon earth, by the tenor of the presents give, concede, and assign for ever to you, and to the kings of Castile
and Leon, your successors, all the islands and main-lands discovered and
which may hereafter be discovered, towards the west and south, with all
their dominions, cities, castles, places, and towns, and with all their rights,
jurisdictions, and appurtenances, whether the lands and islands found or
that shall be found, be situated towards India, or towards any other part
whatsoever; and we make, constitute and depute you, and your foresaid heirs
and successors, lords of them, with full, free and absolute power and authority and jurisdiction : drawing however and fixing a line from the arctic
pole, viz from the north, to the antarctic pole, viz to the south; which line
must be distant from any one of the islands whatsoever, vulgarly called the
Azores, and Cape de Verd Islands, a hundred leagues towards the west and
south ; upon condition that no other Christian King or Prince has actual
possession of any of the islands and main-lands found or that shall be found,
discovered or that shall be discovered from the foresaid line towards the
west and south, until the day of the nativity of our Lord Jesus Christ last
past, from which the present year one thousand four hundred and ninety-
three commences, when some of the foresaid islands were discovered by your
messengers and captains: decreeing nevertheless, that by this our donation,
concession and assignation, it is not intended to take or deprive of the *jus
quæsitum*, any other Christian Prince, who may have actually possessed
the said islands and main-lands up to the aforementioned day of the nativity of our Lord Jesus Christ. And moreover, we command you, by the
holy obedience which you owe us, that (as you promise, and we doubt not
you will perform it, in consequence of your very great devotion, and royal
magnanimity) you appoint to the said main-lands and islands upright men
and fearing God, learned skilful and expert in instructing the foresaid natives and inhabitants in the Catholic faith, and in teaching them good
morals, employing for that purpose all requisite diligence. And we most
strictly forbid every person whatsoever, and of whatsoever dignity, (even
imperial or royal) state, degree, order, or condition they may be, under the
penalty of excommunication *latae sententiae*, which they will incur by the
very fact of transgression, to presume, either for trafficking, or for any other
cause whatsoever, to approach, without special licence from you, and your
foresaid heirs and successors, the islands and main-lands found, or that
shall be found, discovered or that shall be discovered, towards the west and
south, drawing and fixing a line from the arctic to the antarctic pole ; whether the main-lands and islands found, or that shall be found, be towards
India, or towards any other part; which line must be distant from any one
of the islands whatsoever, which are vulgarly called the Azores, and Cape
de Verd, a hundred leagues towards the west and south, as has been said :
notwithstanding the apostolic constitutions and ordinances, and all other
things to the contrary whatsoever. We confide in Him, from whom empires,

dominions and all good things proceed, that the Lord directing your actions, if you prosecute this holy and praiseworthy resolution, in a short time, for the happiness and glory of the whole Christian world, your labours and your efforts will obtain a most happy accomplishment. But, as it would be a difficult thing to present the present letters in each of the places where it might be requisite, we will and decree, of our own similar motion and knowledge, that the copies of them, signed by a public notary, employed for that purpose, and provided with the seal of some person possessed of ecclesiastical dignity, or a member of the ecclesiastical court, be regarded as equally valid in all respects in courts of justice and without, and everywhere else, as if the present letters were exhibited or shewn. Let no person therefore presume to infringe, or with rash boldness to contravene this page of our commendation, exhortation, requisition, donation, concession, assignation, constitution, deputation, decree, mandate, inhibition, and will. For if any person presumes to do so, be it known to him that he will incur the indignation of the Almighty God, and of the blessed apostles Peter and Paul. Given in Rome, at St. Peter's, in the year of the incarnation of our Lord, one thousand four hundred and ninety-three, on the fourth day of May, in the first year of our Pontificate. *Gratis.* (The signatures follow.)

APPENDIX B. (BULL B).

The following is a copy of the Bull " *Eximiae devotionis* " taken from the " *Fonti Italiani*," Part III. By this Bull the Pope granted to Spain, over the territories discovered for the Spanish crown, the same rights which had, by a series of Bulls extending over fifty years, been granted to Portugal over the territories to the south along the coast of Africa and to the eastwards " as far as the Indies." Such rights are conferred upon Spain *en bloc* without enumeration *quoad the territories discovered for Spain* and in doing this the rights of Portugal and the contents of the previous Bulls are of necessity confirmed, *quoad* the territories discovered for Portugal.

This Bull is to be found also in Solorzano, *De Indiarum Jure*, and in Rainaldi, *Annales Ecclesiastici*. It is not in Navarrete, nor is it often referred to in the books; though Herrera in one passage evidently has it in mind, and Barros refers to it. Mr. Harrisse says it is not now to be found in the Spanish Archives. He has given (Diplomatic History) the only English translation which has hitherto appeared. His text was taken from Heywood's *Documenta Selecta*. He thinks Rainaldi gave this Bull a place before the Bull *Inter cetera* by mistake; but Rainaldi made no mistake. This Bull is dated May 3, and Rainaldi never knew of the suppressed *Inter cetera* draft of the same day. He gave the only *Inter cetera* he knew anything about, that dated May 4.

The reader is requested to compare the passages omitted from the draft Bull and given in the footnotes in appendix A with the passages printed in italics in this Bull. He will find that they are almost word for word the same, and all that remains in the Bull beyond this is merely the technical framework of formal verbiage always found in such documents.

ALEXANDER episcopus, servus servorum Dei, carissimo in Christo filio Ferdinando regi et carissimæ in Christo filiæ Helisabeth reginæ Castellæ, Legionis, Aragonum et Granatæ illustribus, salutem et apostolicam benedictionem.

Eximiæ devotionis sinceritas et integra fides, quibus nos et Romanam reveremini Ecclesiam, non indigne merentur ut illa vobis favorabiliter concedamus, per quæ sanctum et laudabile propositum vestrum et opus inceptum in quærendis terris et insulis remotis ac incognitis in dies melius et facilius ad honorem omnipotentis Dei, et imperii christiani propagationem, ac fidei catholicæ exaltationem prosequi valeatis. Hodie siquidem omnes et singulas terras firmas et insulas remotas et incognitas versus partes occidentales et mare Oceanum consistentes, per vos, seu nuntios vestros, ad id propterea non sine magnis laboribus, periculis et impensis destinatos, repertas et reperiendas in posterum, quæ sub actuali dominio temporali aliquorum dominorum christianorum constitutæ non essent, cum omnibus illarum dominiis, civitatibus, castris, locis, villis, juribus et jurisdictionibus universis, vobis hæredibusque et successoribus vestris, Castellæ et Legionis regibus, in perpetuum, motu proprio et ex certa scientia ac de apostolicæ potestatis plenitudine donavimus, concessimus et assignavimus, prout in nostris inde confectis litteris plenius continetur. *Cum autem alias nonnullis Portugalliae regibus qui in partibus Africae, Guineae et Minere auri, ac alias insulas etiam in similibus concessione et donatione apostolica eis facta repererunt et acquisiverunt, per Sedem apostolicam diversa privilegia gratiae, libertates, immunitates exemptiones, facultates, litterae et in-*

dulta concessa fuerint; nos volentes etiam, prout dignum et conveniens existit, vos hæredesque et successores vestros prædictos non minoribus gratiis, prærogativis, et favoribus prosequi, motu simili, non ad vestram vel alterius pro vobis super hoc oblatæ petitionem instantiam, sed de nostra mera liberalitate ac eisdem scientia et apostolicæ potestatis plenitudine, *vobis ac haeredibus et successoribus vestris praedictis, ut in insulis et terris per vos seu nomine vestro hactenus repertis hujusmodi et reperiendis in posterum omnibus et singulis gratiis, privilegiis, exemptionibus, libertatibus, facultatibus, immunitatibus, litteris et indultis regibus Portugalliae concessis hujusmodi, quorum omnium tenores ac si de verbo ad verbum praesentibus insererentur haberi volumus pro sufficienter expressis et insertis, uti, potiri et gaudere libite et licite possitis et debeatis in omnibus et per omnia perinde ac si illa omnia vobis et haeredibus et successoribus vestris praefatis specialiter concessa fuissent, auctoritate apostolica tenore praesentium de specialis dono gratiae indulgemus, illaque in omnibus et per omnia ad vos haeredesque ac successores vestros praedictos extendimus pariter et ampliamus,* ac eisdem motu et forma perpetuo concedimus, non obstantibus constitutionibus et ordinationibus apostolicis, nec non omnibus illis quæ in litteris Portugalliæ regibus concessis hujusmodi concessa sunt, non obstantibus ceterisque contrariis quibuscumque. Verum, quia difficile foret præsentes litteras ad singula quæque loca in quibus expediens fuerit defferri, volumus, ac motu et scientia similibus decernimus, quod illarum transumptis, manu publici notarii inde rogati subscriptis et sigillo alicujus personæ in ecclesiastica dignitate constitutæ, seu curiæ ecclesiasticæ, munitis, ea prorsus fides indubia in judicio et extra ac, alias ubilibet adhibeatur, quæ præsentibus adhiberetur, si essent exhibitæ vel ostensæ. Nulli ergo omnino hominum liceat hanc paginam nostræ exhortationis, requisitionis, donationis, assignationis, investituræ, facti, constitutionis, deputationis, mandati, inhibitionis, nostrorum indulti, extensionis, ampliationis, concessionis, voluntatis et decreti infringere, vel ei ausu temerario contraire. Si quis autem hoc attentare presumpserit, indignationem omnipotentis Dei ac beatorum Petri et Pauli apostolorum ejus se noverit incursurum. Datum Romæ, apud sanctum Petrum, anno incarnationis dominicæ millesimo quadringentesimo nonagesimo tertio, quinto nonas maii, pontificatus nostri anno primo.

TRANSLATION.

Alexander, Bishop, Servant of the Servants of God; to the illustrious sovereigns, our very dear son in Christ, Ferdinand, King, and to our very dear daughter in Christ, Isabella, Queen, of Castile, Leon, Aragon and Granada. Health and apostolic benediction.

The sincerity of distinguished devotion and the soundness of faith, by which you reverence us and the Roman Church, justly deserve that we should approvingly grant you those things which may enable to follow up your holy and praiseworthy purpose, and the enterprise undertaken for seeking out remote and unknown lands and islands, day by day tending more to the glory of Almighty God, the propagation of the kingdom of Christ, and the exaltation of the Catholic faith.

Now, therefore, we, of our own motion from certain knowledge and out of the fulness of apostolic power, have given, conceded and assigned unto you, and your heirs and successors, the Kings of Castile and Leon, in perpetuity, all and singular the remote and unknown mainlands and islands, situated towards the regions of the West and the main ocean, which are not under the actual temporal dominion of some Christian master, discovered and to be hereafter discovered, by you or your emissaries sent for that purpose, not without great labour, danger and expense; together with all their lordships, cities, fortresses, places, farms, rights and jurisdictions, as is set forth more fully in our letters drawn up for that purpose.

And since, at other times, divers privileges, favours, liberties, immunities, exemptions, faculties, letters and indults were conceded, by the apostolic See, to several Kings of Portugal, who, in the regions of Africa, Guinea and the Gold mine, have discovered and acquired other íslands, under similar grant and concession made to them by the Apostolic See; we, desiring to bestow, as is worthy and becoming, also upon you and your heirs and successors aforesaid gifts, prerogatives and favours to a not less extent, of our like motion, not at your instance or that of any other person on your behalf by petition made to us about this matter, but of our own simple liberality and with the same knowledge and fulness of apostolic power grant, by apostolic authority according to the tenor of these presents, by a gift of especial grace, to you and your heirs and successors aforesaid, that, in the islands and lands up to the present time discovered by you or in your name and in future to be discovered, you may use, hold and freely enjoy all and singular the gifts, privileges, exemptions, liberties, faculties, immunities, letters and indults as granted to the Kings of Portugal, the purport of all which grants we ordain shall be held expressed and inserted herein, as sufficiently as if they were recited word by word in these presents, and that you may and should lawfully, in all things and in all respects, so hold them as if they had all been specially conceded to you and your heirs and successors aforesaid; and we extend and enlarge them, in all things and all respects, equally to you and your heirs and successors aforesaid, and we grant them, in the same manner and form, in perpetuity; notwithstanding apostolic constitutions and ordinances and all those things which, in the letters granted to the Kings of Portugal, have been so conceded; and notwithstanding all other things to the contrary.

But, since it would be difficult for these letters to be carried to all places which may be expedient, we will and, with like motion and knowledge, decree that to copies of them, signed by the hand of a public notary employed for that purpose and authenticated by the seal of some official person of ecclesiastical dignity or of an ecclesiastical court, the same entire faith shall be given, in courts of justice and outside them and in all other places, which would be given to these presents if they were exhibited or shown.

Therefore, let no man whomsoever infringe this charter of our exhortation, requisition, donation, assignment, investiture, deed, constitution, allotment, concession, will and decree, or, with rash audacity, contravene it. But if anyone should presume to make the attempt, be it known to him that he will incur the indignation of Almighty God and of the blessed apostles Peter and Paul.

Given at Rome, at St. Peter's, in the year of the incarnation of Our Lord, 1493, on the third day of May, in the first year of our pontificate.

APPENDIX C. (BULL D).

Bull said to have been issued by Alexander VI. and dated September 25, 1493, as printed in the "Fonti Italiani." No trace of any original having been found, it was copied into that collection from Solorzano " De Indiarum Jure," Madrid, 1629. The Latin version is supposed to be a re-translation by Solorzano from a Spanish version made by one of the secretaries of Philip II., A.D. 1554.

ALEXANDER episcopus, servus servorum Dei, charissimo in Christo filio Ferdinando regi et charissimæ in Christo filiæ Helizabeth reginæ Castellæ, Legionis, Aragonum et Granatæ, illustribus, salutem et apostolicam benedictionem. Dudum siquidem omnes et singulas insulas et terras firmas inventas et inveniendas versus occidentem et meridiem, quæ sub actuali dominio temporali aliquorum dominorum christianorum constitutæ non essent, vobis heredibusque et successoribus vestris Castellæ et Legionis regibus in perpetuum motu proprio et de certa scientia ac de apostolicæ potestatis plenitudine donavimus, concessimus et assignavimus : vosque ac heredes et successores prefatos de illis investimus ; illarumque dominos cum plena, libera et omnimoda potestate, auctoritate et jurisdictione constituimus et deputavimus, prout in nostris inde confectis litteris, quarum tenorem, ac si de verbo ad verbum præsentibus insererentur, haberi volumus pro sufficienter expressis, plenius continetur. Cum autem contingere posset quod nuntii et capitanei aut vassalli vestri versus occidentem et meridiem navigantes, ad partes orientales applicarent, ac insulas et terras firmas, quæ inde fuissent vel essent, reperirent, nos volentes etiam vos favoribus prosequi gratiosis, motu et scientia ac potestatis apostolicæ plenitudine similibus, donationem, concessionem, assignationem et litteras prædictas, cum omnibus et singulis in eisdem litteris contentis clausulis ad omnes et singulas insulas et terras firmas inventas et inveniendas, ac detectas et detegendas, quæ, navigando aut itinerando versus occidentem aut meridiem hujusmodi sint vel fuerint aut apparuerint, sive in partibus occidentalibus vel meridionalibus et orientalibus et Indiæ existant, auctoritate apostolica, tenore præsentium in omnibus et per omnia, perinde ac si in litteris prædictis de eis plena et expressa mentio facta fuisset, extendimus pariter et ampliamus. Vobis et hæredibus et successoribus vestris prædictis per vos, vel alium seu alios, corporalem insularum ac terrarum prædictarum possessionem propria auctoritate libere apprehendendi ac perpetuo retinendi, illasque adversus quoscumque impedientes etiam defendendi, plenam et liberam facultatem concedentes, ac quibuscumque personis etiam cujuscumque dignitatis, status, gradus, ordinis vel conditionis, sub excommunicationis latæ sententiæ, pena, quam contrafacientes eo ipso incurrant, districtius inhibentes, ne ad partes prædictas ad navigandum, piscandum, vel inquirendum insulas vel terras firmas, aut quovis alio respectu seu colore, ire, vel mittere quoquomodo præsumant, absque expressa vel speciali vestra ac hæredum et successorum prædictorum licentia. Non obstantibus constitutionibus et ordinationibus apostolicis, ac quibusvis donationibus, concessionibus, facultatibus et assignationibus per nos vel prædecessores nostros, quibuscunque, regibus vel principibus, infantibus, aut quibusvis aliis personis, aut ordinibus et militiis de prædictis partibus, maribus, insulis atque terris, vel aliqua eorum parte, ex quibusvis causis, etiam pietatis vel fidei aut redemptionis captivorum, et aliis quantumcunque urgentissimis, et cum quibusvis clausulis etiam derogatoriarum derogatoriis, fortioribus, efficacioribus et insolitis, etiam quascunque sententias, censuras et penas in se continentibus, quæ suum per actualem et realem possessionem non essent sortitæ effectum, licet forsan aliquando illi quibus donationes et concessiones hujusmodi factæ fuissent, aut eorum nuntii, ibidem navigassent. Quos tenores illarum etiam præsentibus pro sufficienter expressis et insertis habentes, motu, scientia et potestatis plenitudine similibus omnino revocamus, ac quoad terras et insulas per eos actualiter non possessas pro infectis haberi volumus, necnon omnibus illis quæ in litteris prædictis voluimus non obstare, ceterisque contrariis quibuscunque.

Datum Romæ, apud sanctum Petrum, anno incarnationis dominicæ millesimo quadringentesimo nonagesimo tertio. Sexto kalendas octobris, pontificatus nostri anno secundo.

TRANSLATION.

Alexander, Bishop, Servant of the Servants of God, to the illustrious sovereigns, his very dear son in Christ Ferdinand, the king, and to his very dear daughter in Christ, Isabella, the queen of Castile, Leon, Aragon and Granada—Health and apostolic benediction.

Whereas, a while ago, we, of our mere will, certain knowledge and in the fulness of our apostolic power, gave, conceded and assigned, in perpetuity, to you and your heirs and successors, the kings of Castile and Leon, all and singular the islands and mainlands discovered or to be discovered, towards the west and south, which were not under the actual temporal dominion of some Christian master; with these we invest you and your heirs and successors aforesaid; and we have constituted and appointed you as lords of those regions, with full, free and entire power, authority and jurisdiction, as set forth more fully in our letters drawn up for that purpose; the purport of which letters we ordain to be held as completely expressed as if they were recited in these present letters, word for word.

Since, moreover, it may happen that your emissaries, captains, or vassals, when sailing towards the west and south, may turn towards the eastern regions and find islands and mainlands which are, or were, to that quarter pertaining ; wishing to follow up our gracious favours to you by similar favours, we, of our will, knowledge and fulness of apostolic power, equally extend and enlarge, with apostolic authority, by the tenor of these presents, in everything and in all respects, the same as if in the aforesaid letters full and express mention had been made of them, the donation, concession, assignment and letters aforesaid, with all and singular the clauses contained in the same letters, to apply to all and singular the islands and mainlands found and to be found, discovered and to be discovered, which in sailing or journeying in this manner towards the west or south may be, or shall be, or shall appear, whether they actually are in western or in southern and eastern regions or in India.

Granting to you and to your heirs and successors aforesaid, the full and free faculty of taking and perpetually holding, freely of your own authority, by yourselves or by another or others, bodily possession of the aforesaid islands and lands, and also of defending them against all persons who may obstruct; and most strictly prohibiting all persons soever, even of any dignity soever, or status, rank, order, or condition, under penalty of excommunication (latæ sententiæ) which transgressors by the very act will incur, from presuming to go, or send, to the said part, to navigate, fish, or seek out islands or mainlands, under any pretext, without the special and express license of you and your aforesaid heirs.

Notwithstanding constitutions and apostolic ordinances and any donations, concessions, faculties and assignments, made by ourselves or our predecessors to all persons whomsover; to kings or princes, to persons of royal houses (infantibus), or any other persons, to regular orders and to military orders, for the aforesaid regions, seas, islands and lands or for any part of them, without regard to the causes of the grant, even if for objects of piety, or of religion, or of redeeming captives or to other causes of the most urgent nature, and with clauses of whatever kind, even derogations of derogations the strongest most efficacious and unusual, and containing judgments, censures and penalties of any kind which have not come into effect by means of actual and real possession, even supposing that, at some time, those to whom donations and concessions of this nature have been made or their emissaries may have sailed there.

Moreover, holding that the tenor of those letters are sufficiently expressed and inserted in these presents, we revoke them altogether by similar will, knowledge and apostolic power and we will them to be held as never made, in so far as they refer to lands and islands not actually in possession, and so we have decreed notwithstanding everything in the aforesaid letters and all other things to the contrary.

Given at St. Peter's at Rome in the year of our Lord 1493, on Sept. 25th, and in the second year of our pontificate.

APPENDIX D.

Correspondence between the Sovereigns of Spain and Jaime Ferrer concerning the position and the best manner of laying down the line of demarcation of the treaty of Tordesillas, signed June 7, 1494. Extracted from Navarrete *Coleccion de los Viajes*, vol. 2, p. 111. Translated with the aid of an official expert translator of Spanish.

January 27, 1495.

To the very high and very puissant Sovereigns of Spain, &c., by the grace of God our very righteous lords.

Very high and very powerful Sovereigns: Don Juan de la Nussa, Lieutenant of your Highnesses, has twice shown me some instructions in which your Highnesses make known the decision regarding the partition your Highnesses have made with the most illustrious king of Portugal upon the Ocean, starting from Cape Verde in a westerly line for a distance of three hundred and seventy leagues; and therefore, very high and most sereno Sovereigns, I have examined (the subject) to the extent of my humble understanding, although late, and not so soon as I had wished, on account of a slight illness; and therefore I send to your Highnesses, by a man of mine, a figure of the world on a large scale on which may be seen the two hemispheres, to wit, our Arctic and the opposite Antarctic one. And likewise you will see the equinoctial circle and the two tropics of the declination of the sun, and the seven climates, and each one of these circles put in its proper place as in the *treatise on the sphere* and in the *situ orbis* learned men direct and divide into degrees. And, in order that the distance may more clearly be seen of the said three hundred and seventy leagues and how far they extend in a westerly line starting from the said Cape Verde, I have intersected the said distance from pole to pole with red lines, which at the equator are twenty-three degrees apart, and with acute angles, the said lines correspond to the poles of the earth in this figure :—

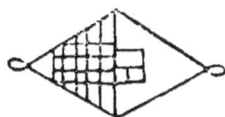

and all that is crossed by yellow lines will be what belongs to the most illustrious King of Portugal, turning in the direction of the Antarctic pole. And this distance of sea completes the said three hundred and seventy leagues which are, as I said above, twenty-three degrees starting from Cape Verde in a westerly line.

And if in connection with this decision (treaty of partition) your Highnesses should command that I should go thither (to Cape Verde) I will, of my great and obedient love, certainly go at my own expense and without any pay. And in very truth my desire is that all I have in this world shall be at the service of your Royal Highnesses—whom may the infinite Trinity ever keep in guard and protection with very long and very prosperous life.

From Barcelona, January 27, 1495.

Their Catholic Majesties did not understand the above letter, and indeed, if the little figure above may be taken as an indication of what was on the map sent, it is not to be wondered at. Ferrer counted the distance as from Cape Verde, whereas it was from the islands off that cape, and he made the

370 leagues equal to twenty-three degrees, or 16'¦₁₁ leagues to each degree on that parallel. Very soon after (Feb. 28) their Majesties wrote as follows :

BY THE KING AND THE QUEEN—TO JAIME FERRER, THEIR SUBJECT.

·THE KING AND THE QUEEN. Jaime Ferrer. We saw your letter and the inclosure you sent us therein, which seems to us very good. We consider your having sent it as a service; but for the understanding of it, it is necessary you should be here, and, for our service, that you should put your coming into effect so that you shall be here at latest on the first of May. In which you will do us service.

From Madrid on the 28th day of February, 1495.

I THE KING—I THE QUEEN.

By order of the King and Queen.

Joan de la Parra.

There is no date attached to the following formal opinion. but, taken in connection with the preceding letters, it must have been presented sometime during the first half of 1495. It also is in Navarrete (Vol. 2, p. 113) as follows. The calculations and the nautical statements in sections 4 to 6 do not impress the reader with a high opinion of Ferrer's attainments; but that may partly be accounted for by errors in copying or printing.

The opinion and judgment of Mossen Jaume Ferrer regarding the Treaty made between the Most Catholic Sovereigns and the King of Portugal ; in which is shown that the author was a great cosmographer and a wonderful expert on the sea.

1. The manner of determining the terminus or end of the three hundred and seventy leagues, starting from the Islands of Cape Verde on a westerly line is as follows :

2. First, it must be noted that the said Cape Verde and its islands lie fifteen degrees from the equator, and it is likewise to be noted that the said 370 leagues, starting from the said islands, comprise to the west eighteen degrees, and each degree on that parallel contains twenty leagues and five-eighths. Moreover, it is necessary to make a straight line, in latitude (sic) from pole to pole only in this our hemisphere, intersecting the said parallel exactly at the end of the said eighteen degrees; and everything lying within this line on the left hand, turning towards the side of Guinea, will belong to the King of Portugal, and the other part by the West as far as it turns by the East towards the Arabian Gulf will belong to the Kings our Lords, if their ships first sail thither. And this is what I understand by the treaty made by your Highnesses with the King of Portugal.

3. And a truth it is and a chief principle in cosmography that in sailing on one same parallel the said terminus can never be ascertained by means of the elevation of the Pole-star (Polus mundi); and the reason is this, that in sailing always by the same parallel the said Pole-star (Polus) maintains the same elevation through all the circumference of the said parallel. And that is true.

4. Nevertheless, I say, that it is possible and a very certain thing that the said terminus and extremity of the said 370 leagues can be ascertained by the North star by the following rule and practical method.

It is necessary for the vessel leaving the Cape Verde islands in search of the said terminus to leave the western parallel or line upon the left hand and to take her course by the quarter of the West towards the Northwest, and to continue to sail in that direction until the Pole-star rises eighteen degrees and one-third, and then the said vessel will be exactly on the aforesaid line which passes from pole to pole at the extremity of the 370 leagues. And from there it is necessary that the said vessel change and take her course along said line in the direction of the Antarctic pole up to that point where the Arctic pole is fifteen degrees in elevation, and then at that exact end will be the end of the line or parallel which passes through the said Cape Verde and at the end and true terminus of the said 370 leagues; which terminus is very clearly indicated by the elevation of the North star according to the aforesaid rule.

5. And because the sailing chart is not wholly useful and does not suffice for the mathematical demonstration of the above rule, a world map in spherical form is necessary, divided into two hemispheres by its lines and degrees, and the situation of the land, islands and sea, each in its own place—which world map I put down together with these expressions of my meaning and opinion, the more clearly to demonstrate the truth.

And I say that to understand the above rule and practical method it is necessary to be a cosmographer, arithmetician and navigator, or to understand the art; and he who does not possess all these three sciences, cannot possibly understand (the rule) nor (can he succeed) by any other way or rule if he is not expert in the three said sciences.

6. And for a further exposition of the above rule it must be known that the quarter of the wind (point of the compass) the vessel takes as its course, starting from the Cape Verde islands at the end of the 370 leagues, will be distant from the western parallel or line seventy-four leagues at the rate of twenty per cent, and because the said quarter (of the wind-rose or compass) inclines towards the North sailing by it the different (increasing) elevation of the pole-star is clearly apparent, and the said seventy-four leagues comprise three degrees and a third of latitude, very nearly.

7. It is, moreover, to be noted that pursuing the above rule it is necessary to give to each degree seven hundred stadia, according to Strabo, Alfragano, Teodoci, Macrobi, Ambrosi and Euristhenes (Eratosthenes) ; since Ptolemy gives only five hundred stadia to a degree. And I say further that there is another method of finding the said terminus according to the practice and science of mariners, and it is as follows.

8. First, let the sovereigns our lords and the King of Portugal take twenty mariners, ten for each side, the best to be found, and conscientious men, and let them start in one vessel from the Cape Verde islands on a westerly line, and let each one of the said mariners note with great care on his chart, every six hours, the course the vessel makes according to his judgment; and, having been bound under oath, let none of them communicate his opinion to another until the first of the mariners who in his judgment finds himself at the said terminus shall state so to two captains—men of reputation, put on board the said vessel by the will and accord of the said sovereigns. And let the said captains then take the opinions and judgments of the other mariners and, if the rest agree with the first who finds himself at the terminus, let them take his decision as conclusive and final as to the said terminus; and if they do not agree with the first, let them take the opinion and judgment of the majority, and after agreeing, let them change the course on a straight line towards the Antarctic pole, and everything they find on the left hand towards Guinea shall belong to the King of Portugal in the manner above stated.

This second method is uncertain and may be erroneous because it is based on the simple and sole judgment and opinion of mariners, and the first rule is very certain, (that one) by the elevation of the North star, as is shown above.

9. And if in this my decision and opinion any error appear, I will always defer to the correction of those who know and understand more than I, especially to the Admiral of the Indies, who at the present time knows more than any other person in this subject, for he is greatly learned in the theory and admirably practical, as his famous achievements demonstrate ; and I believe that Divine Providence holds him as elect to carry out its great mystery and service in this undertaking, which I believe is the disposition and preparation of that (result) which, hereafter, the same Divine Providence will manifest to its great glory—the salvation and good of the world.

10. Here is shown the navigation of the Admiral of the Main-land. Ptolemy in the eighth book *de situ orbis* says at chapter five:

That the true circumference of the earth at the equator is 180,000 stades, at the rate of five hundred stades to a degree according to his calculation, and counting eight stades per mile, are 22,500 miles, which are 5,625 leagues at the rate of four miles per league in Castillian reckoning, each degree coming to fifteen leagues and two hundred and twenty-five parts of three hundred and sixty. And in the same Book, chapter five, he says that the circle of the tropics is 164,672 stades, which are 20,584 miles, and 5,146 leagues, making for each degree fourteen leagues and one hundred and six parts of three hundred and sixty. Moreover, according to Strabo, Alfragano, Ambrosi, Macrobi, Teodosi and Euristhenes, the said circumference of the earth is 252,000 stades, the which 252,000 stades, at the rate of eight stades per mile, are 31,500 miles, and at four miles per league, are 7,875 leages. Item :—By the circle of the tropics the circumference is 7,204 leagues and seventy-two thousand parts of one hundred and eighty thousand; and I decided it by the rule of three, saying if 22,500 miles at the equator according to Ptolemy give me 7,875 for the said equator, what will 20,584 miles of the circle of the tropics give me ? And in this way you will arrive at the above 7,204 and a half leagues almost, according to the said learned men.

The said circle of the tropics is shorter than the equinoctial circle by 670½ leagues, which is, at four miles per league, 2,682 miles, according to the above calculation summed up and proved throughout. That is, however, calculating according as the above-mentioned learned men direct, 700 stades to a degree; although Ptolemy allows no more than 500 stades to a degree, as above said in the already mentioned book, de situ orbis.

11. Item :—It is to be noted that on the equinoctial circle each degree has twenty-one leagues and five parts of eight, and on the tropics each degree has twenty leagues and four parts of three hundred and sixty, according to the said learned men.

12. Starting from Cape Verde on a westerly line the terminus three hundred and seventy leagues comprises eighteen degrees, inasmuch as the said line or parallel is fifteen degrees distant from the equator, and therefore the degrees each of them contains twenty leagues and five parts of eight, according to the said learned men.

13. From Cape Verde to the Grand Canary island are 232 leagues of four miles per league, and it lies from the said Canary on a meridian almost at a third of the "lebeix" or southwestern quarter, and is distant fifteen degrees from the equator, and the middle island of those which lie in front of Cape Verde lies in the quarter of the West towards the Northwest 117 leagues (away), which are equal to five degrees and two-thirds; and from this middle island commences the terminus of the 370 leagues towards the West which terminus is eighteen degrees towards the West from the said middle island, and on that parallel each degree is twenty leagues and five parts of eight, counting 700 stades to a degree, according to the above cited learned men, although Ptolemy uses a different calculation.

14. And according to Ptolemy, each degree of the equator contains fifteen leagues and two-thirds, and of the tropics fourteen leagues and one-third, and on the parallel of Cape Verde fourteen leagues and two-thirds, and therefore the 370 leagues upon that parallel are understood as extending to the West twenty-five degrees and one-third nearly.

15. And the Admiral says in his letter that Cape Verde is nine and a quarter degrees distant from the equator. According to Ptolemy, I see him allowing fifteen and two-thirds leagues to a degree ; nevertheless, I decide with the other learned men as to the distance of the said islands from the equator. The division into stades, although the number given by Ptolemy is different from that given by the above cited learned men, Strabo, Alfragano, Macrobi, Teodosi, and Euristhenes, they are all essentially in agrement, because Ptolemy makes use of longer stades; so that his 180,000 stades are equal to the 252,000 stades of the above mentioned learned men for the equinoctial line as above said.

APPENDIX E.

The table on the next page has been drawn up on the universally accepted basis of the old navigators and geographers, viz., 8 stades equal to 1 Roman mile, and 4 Roman miles equal to 1 Italian league. To attempt mathematical exactness would fill it with confusing fractions and make it useless in reading the old authors. As an illustration of the near approximation of these equivalents let the last item be taken in the third column. If the 20,400 Italian miles be multiplied by 1,618 yards and divided by 2,029 yards and thus reduced into nautical miles, the result would be 16,268 nautical miles against the 16,320 nautical miles of the reckoning in the table by means of stades. The difference is thus only fifty-two miles in the whole circumference of the earth. This will give the measure of the discrepancy or non-equivalence of the quantities.

NOTES TO APPENDIX E.

a. Eratosthenes made the circumference to be 250,000 stades, and added 2,000 stades for convenience of division by 360 into degrees without fractions.

b. Jaimo Ferrer (see Appendix D) is reported, as the opinion is given in Navarrete, to have stated that a degree of the equator is 21⅔ leagues; but if the circumference of 7875 leagues, given also in the same opinion, be divided by 360, the result will be 21⅞ leagues. There is, therefore, an error in the text or in Ferrer's arithmetic.

c. Posidonius.—I have followed Mons. D'Avezac and Sir George Cornewall Lewis in giving 240,000 stades as the measure of the earth's circumference fixed upon by Posidonius. In most books it is given as 180,000, on the authority of Strabo. It is certain, however, that his first opinion was in favour of 240,000 stades. This statement is made by his admirer Cleomenes, who knew of no other figures. Historiaus reconcile the conflicting statements by assuming that he changed his opinion in later life.

d. Pytheas of Massilia was a navigator [explorer or merchant], who about the time of Alexander the Great visited the north of Europe. He passed outside the Pillars of Hercules, and sailed in the British seas. Polybius and Strabo considered him to be an impostor, who palmed off his imaginary adventures for truth; but the great Greek geographers accepted his statements so far as to make up their maps on his information. Sir George Cornewall Lewis [*Astronomy of the Ancients*, p. 467], following his naturally sceptical temperament, is inclined to reject his voyages; while, on the other hand, the uncritical optimism of Lelewel accepts them fully. The truth lies, probably, between these extremes; for certain it is that Pytheas was a man of great enterprise and unusual powers of observation. He fixed the latitude of Massilia, by means of a gnomon, at 43° 3′ 58″, and as it is in reality 43° 17′ 30″, it is a very remarkable observation to have been made 224° years ago, and there are very few latitudes so nearly correct in all the ancient authors. Hipparchus accepted the latitude of Massilia as fixed by Pytheas; but when he himself calculated by the gnomon the latitude of Byzantium he fixed it to be the same as Massilia, two degrees out of the truth. The "impostor" had made a more correct determination than the greatest of the Greek astronomers. Pytheas, when in the British seas, saw the tides which, on the west coast of Britain, are very high in the estuaries of the rivers, and are phenomena most striking to one from the tideless shores of the Mediterranean. He, moreover, correctly attributed them to the influence of the moon.

The particular interest of Pytheas, in relation to the subject of this paper, is the belief of Lelewel that he estimated a degree to be 600 stades—almost the exact equivalent of 60 geographical miles. Pytheas does not, however, appear to have made any direct statement to that effect. It is an inference from his estimation of the distance between Orcus in 61° and Thule in 66°, which was also given as six days' sail directly north, or 3000 stades. The figures are rounded out too much to be made the basis of serious calculation.

e. Magellan gave this opinion to King Ferdinand just before sailing on his great voyage in A.D. 1518.

f. Enciso.—See *ante,* p. 511, for a discussion of Enciso's opinions.

g. This was, in fact, the opinion of both Spanish and Portuguese navigators and diplomatists whenever the leagues of the treaty of Tordesillas came up for discussion subsequent to the convention at Badajoz.

COMPARATIVE TABLE, in Olympic stades, Italian leagues, Italian miles and modern geographical or nautical miles of the length of the Equator and of a degree of a great circle of the Earth, as accepted by the chief geographical authorities in ancient and mediæval times and at the period of the discovery of America.

AUTHORITIES	STADES Equatorial circumference	STADES Each degree	Nautical miles Equatorial circumference	Nautical miles Each degree	ITALIAN LEAGUES Equatorial circumference	ITALIAN LEAGUES Each degree	ITALIAN MILES Equatorial circumference	ITALIAN MILES Each degree
Estimations in excess of truth.								
Aristotle ...... B.C. 342	400,000	1111·1	40,000	111·1	12,500	34·7	50,000	138·8
Archimedes ...... B.C. 214	300,000	833·3	30,000	83·3	9,375	26·0	37,500	104·1
a. Eratosthenes ...... B.C. 240								
Hipparchus ...... B.C. 160								
Strabo ...... B.C. 24	252,000	700·0	25,200	70	7,875	21·875	31,500	87·5
Pliny ...... A.D. 52								
b. Jaime Ferrer ...... A.D. 1481								
c. Posidonius ...... B.C. 86	240,000	666·6	24,000	66·6	7,500	20·8	30,000	83·3
d. Pytheas of Marseilles ...... B.C. 340	?	?	?	?	?	?	?	?
Present estimate (for comparison)......	**216,000**	**600**	**21,600**	**60**	**6,750**	**18·75**	**27,000**	**75**
Estimations below the truth.								
e. Magellan ...... A.D. 1518								
f. Enciso (practical opinion) ...... A.D. 1519								
Sebastian Cabot (at Badajoz) ...... A.D. 1524								
Thomas Duran (at Badajoz) ...... A.D. 1524	201,600	560	20,160	56	6,300	17·5	25,200	70
Juan Vespucci (at Badajoz) ...... A.D. 1524								
g. Saragossa Convention ...... A.D. 1527								
Champlain ...... A.D. 1632								
g. Spain and Portugal convention ...... A.D. 1681								
Opinion, circa A.D. 1500, in round numbers of Italian leagues and miles	192,000	533·3	19,200	53·33	6,000	16·66	24,000	66·66
c. Posidonius (later opinion)...... B.C.								
Marinus of Tyre, circa ...... A.D. 120	180,000	500	18,000	50	5,625	15·625	22,500	62·5
Ptolemy, circa ...... A.D. 150								
Opinions based on Arabian measurements.								
Friar Bacon ...... A.D. 1267								
Cardinal D'Ailly ...... A.D. 1410	163,200	453·33	16,320	45·33	5,100	14·17	20,400	56·67
Christopher Columbus ...... A.D. 1492								
Fernan Columbus ...... A.D. 1524